The Work of the Sea,
Rivers and Ice

ISBN 0 7175 0791 2

This is a revised combined edition of the three previous
books by R. Kay Gresswell: *Beaches and Coastlines, Rivers and
Valleys* and *Glaciers and Glaciation*.
Published 1978 by Hulton Educational Publications Ltd.,
Raans Road, Amersham, Bucks.

Printed and bound in Great Britain by
Morrison & Gibb Ltd., London and Edinburgh

The Work of the Sea, Rivers and Ice

R. KAY GRESSWELL, M.A., Ph.D.

and

G. R. P. LAWRENCE, M.Sc.

HULTON EDUCATIONAL PUBLICATIONS

Contents

Introduction: Physical Geography

Fig. 1 Layers of sedimentary rock in Wenlock Limestone, south of Much Wenlock

The study of physical geography is one of great variety since it is concerned with the most fundamental aspect of all landscape studies—the shaping of the scenery. The physical geographer (or geomorphologist) is therefore concerned with the materials or rocks which comprise this scenery and how the landform has evolved. The geologist, too, is interested in the rocks, although his concern is more with the materials themselves.

The materials of the landscape are the various rocks and in order to begin to understand the reasons for the many different landforms which exist it is necessary to distinguish between three major rock classes: sedimentary, igneous and metamorphic.

Sedimentary rocks

There are those rocks which are called sedimentary rocks. They are, quite simply, sediments. They consist of grains of sand or mud, and sometimes even of pebbles, which have been dropped on the bottom of the sea at the mouth of a river or in some such place. Sometimes they may have accumulated on the floor of a lake. Since they were so deposited, the particles have become cemented together, generally by lime, and have become hard, solid rock. This may have happened several hundred millions of years ago. Geologists tell us that the Cambrian rocks that form part of Wales are more than 500 million years old; that the limestone of the Pennines is about 300 million years old; and the chalk of the North and South Downs is 120 million.

Since the rocks have been formed as sediments, they have been lifted above the level of the water by earth-movements. Earth-movements have brought the rocks out of the sea, and made them into dry land.

As soon as these rocks come above the water-level, they come within the zone of interest of the geomorphologist. For immediately they do so, or, in fact, just before they emerge, they come under the action of those agents which are going to destroy them. They experience, first, the attack of the sea waves, and then, when the rocks actually do come above water-level, they are exposed to the rain, to snow (if the climate is of that kind), to the action of wind, to the disintegrating action of plant roots, and so on. They have to contend with all the processes which break up the solid rock, and which move it eventually back again to the sea.

The sedimentary rocks which we may examine may be mudstones or siltstones, sandstones, or what the geologist calls conglomerates, that is, made of pebbles. They may even consist only of the remains of animals which lived in the sea, and be chalk and limestone. Whichever they are, they are all sedimentary rocks and they all are at least second-hand, and may even be third-hand, fourth-hand or have been remade even more often than that. The sense in which they are at least second-hand will be made clear later.

Igneous rocks

The second class is the igneous rocks. This is the general name given to all rocks which have come from the interior of the Earth into the position where we find them, in a liquid or molten state—molten, because they were hot.

They are subdivided into two other main types, volcanic rocks and plutonic rocks.

Volcanic rocks such as lava, which issues from volcanoes, and basalt, which flows out of cracks in the Earth's crust, have all come to the surface in a liquid state, and have solidified when they were exposed to the air. They have cooled quickly, and so their crystals are fairly small. The plutonic rocks have also come in a molten state to where we find them, but they solidified before they reached the surface. They solidified while still surrounded by other rocks that already existed, and so therefore they cooled down slowly. As a consequence of this the crystals of which they are composed are very much larger than those of the volcanic rocks. In many instances, during the ages that have passed by since the plutonic rocks were formed, the older rocks that lay above them have been eroded away. That is why we can now often see plutonic rocks at the surface today, although they were formed well beneath. Granite is an example.

Fig. 2 An igneous rock: piece of coarse granite (about $\frac{1}{3}$ size)

(*Miss P. Aylott*)

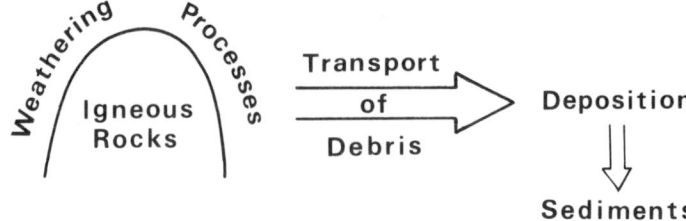

Fig. 3 Diagrammatic representation of rock cycle from igneous to sedimentary

6

The first rocks

The rocks which made the first hard crust of the Earth after its formation were naturally all igneous rocks. The first sedimentary rocks must have been made by the action of the various physical processes on these igneous rocks. The igneous rocks would have to be broken up and transported to the sea, to be redeposited and become the first sedimentary rocks of the world. They, therefore, straight away, must have been second-hand as we said.

Then when these sedimentary rocks had been lifted above the water-level, the same erosive processes acted upon them in their turn, they were broken up, transported to the sea, and again formed fresh sedimentary rocks. Those, then, are third-hand. And so the story has continued ever since. New sedimentary rocks have always been formed from the break-up of the old. And, from time to time, molten material has come from the interior to form additional volcanic and plutonic rocks.

Rocks that changed

There is one other main class into which geologists divide their rocks. They are the rocks which are grouped under the general title of metamorphic rocks.

We are all quite familiar with the phrase 'metamorphosis of insects', which refers most often to the change of a caterpillar into a butterfly or moth. In the same way, metamorphic rocks are either sedimentary or igneous rocks that have been changed since they have been formed. They are generally changed by the action of intense pressure in that part of the Earth's crust, combined very often with a sliding action.

This type of metamorphism is known as dynamic metamorphism, and slate is an example of a rock of this type. Slate, as you know, splits into quite thin layers. The directions in which it splits are not the original layers of the sedimentary rock that it once was. They result from what is called cleavage, caused by this intense sliding pressure.

The second common way in which metamorphism occurs is by the rock getting rather deep in the Earth's crust at some time after it has been formed, and being baked by the heat of the interior of the Earth. In that way chalk and limestone are converted into marble, for example.

Those are the three main classes of rocks with which we are concerned, and we should remember that we can generally recognize a sedimentary rock by the fact that it is in layers, or strata. These are the separate layers of sand and mud that were laid down in the river estuary in which it was formed.

Tilted rocks

Since that time the strata have been lifted above the surface of the water by earth-movements, as we have already mentioned, and, of course, there is no particular reason why they should have been lifted without any tilting.

If two people carried a table across the floor of a room, it is probable that one of them would lift one end higher than the other. The table would no longer be level. So, when layers of rock are lifted above the sea by earth-movements, very often they are inclined, and one may find the rocks at any angle, even vertical, sometimes overturned. Thus we are not surprised when we find sedimentary rocks with their layers tilted (see Fig. 4).

Geomorphology begins

As soon as the rocks come out of the sea, geomorphology begins. At that moment the rocks are exposed to the atmosphere. Rain falls on the rocks. Water from the rain seeps in through the pores or through the minute cracks, called joints, which have occurred in the rocks. The water may freeze, and as it turns to ice, prise these cracks and pore spaces wider open.

Rivers may flow across the rock, and gradually wash it away, or glaciers may pass over it and grind out great U-shaped valleys, but the sea, too, is constantly in contact with the land: either attacking it or building beaches. This zone of contact between land and water is perhaps the most dramatic and will be discussed in the first section of this book.

Fig. 4 Tilted layers north of Barrow-in-Furness

Section One:

The Work of the Sea

1　Waves

The subject is coastlines and the tool that shapes them is, in most cases, waves.

It is surprising how many of us have the idea that waves have something to do with tides. We imagine that one is caused by the other. We stand by the edge of the water on the seashore, and look at the waves as they break in front of us, and some of us say we can see the tide coming in. We cannot, just by watching the waves. The waves look the same whatever the tide is doing. The only way we can tell that the tide is rising is by the fact that the water slowly covers more and more of the beach. Then if we are standing by the waterline, we gradually have to retreat as it advances. Waves have nothing whatever to do with tides, and are produced only by the wind.

Producing a wave

When wind passes over a stretch of water, whether it be the ocean or just a river or lake, the moving air rubs on the water surface. This causes friction. It acts like a brake on the lowermost layers of the air. It slows them down a little. The air layers a few centimetres higher are not hindered in this way and so they continue on at their full speed. Thus they overtake the lower layers. This causes much confusion in the air movement, with the result that it becomes quite irregular. The technical word for this is **turbulence**.

If we imagine the lowest levels of air to be divided into, say, four layers, as shown in Fig. 6, it is clear that the four spots of air represented by the left-hand arrows will not be exactly above one another when they reach the right-hand position. This means that the separate layers of air are sliding on one another. Each upper layer moves a little faster than the one underneath it. There is friction inside

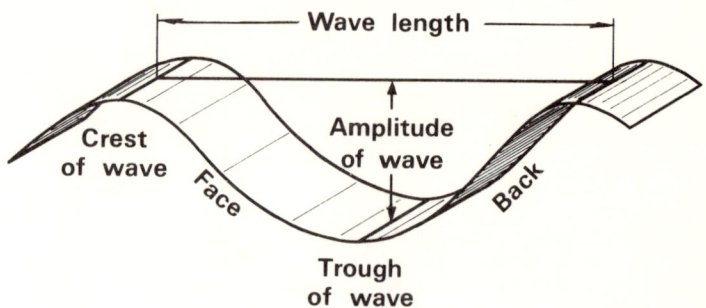

Fig. 5 Technical names

the air itself. This makes the layers tumble head over heels as shown at the right-hand side of the diagram. The process repeats itself time and time again, and a whole tumbled series of whirlpools of air is created, rolling along the water surface like acrobats performing a series of somersaults.

This means that some of the air is no longer moving along a level path, horizontally. Some is moving upwards a little, perhaps even for a metre or so. Some is moving downwards, and this part of the air presses on the water

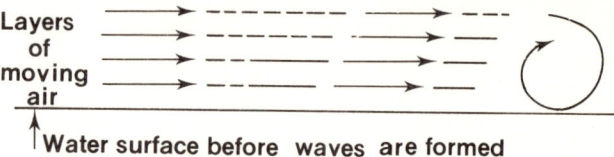

Fig. 6 Friction causes turbulence in the air

A wave starts ....

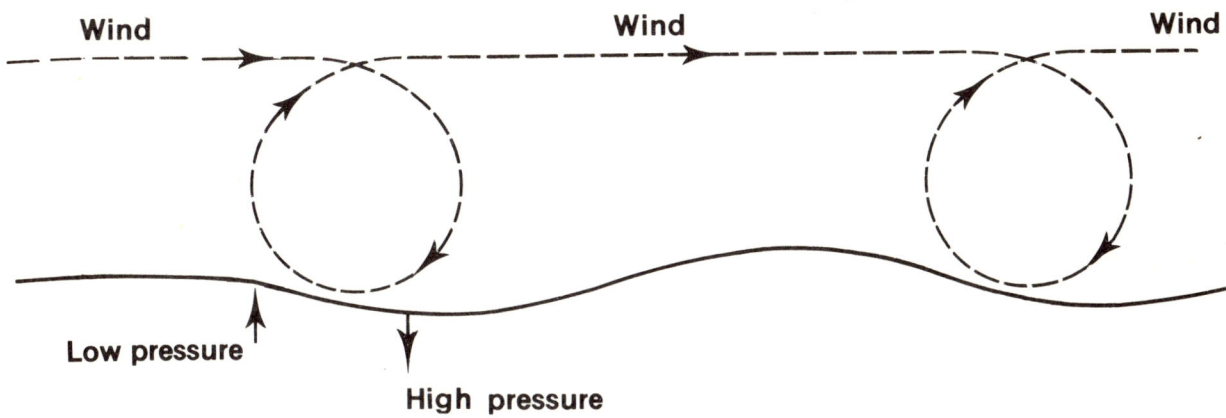

Low pressure

High pressure

Fig. 7 Pressure differences cause waves

below it, so that that part of the surface of the water is pushed down a little. In the same way, the water under the air that is rising upwards is sucked up a little and that part of the water surface rises (Fig. 7). The surface of the sea or lake becomes uneven, and a small wave is produced.

Waves grow

When the turbulence in the air has once made the surface of the sea uneven in this way, it is a fairly easy matter for the wind to build up the small ripples into larger ripples, and then into waves. As it moves onwards, the air finds that it is pressing on the rising slope of the back of one of the ripples, and not only does the wind then play on this and force the shape to move forwards along the surface of the sea, but also it begins to heap it up into a higher mound of water than before. Thus, by this pressure from behind, the wave is both forced to move along and to increase in size.

There is also the backwards moving air due to the turbulence. This actually tries to force some of the surface water to move backwards with it. This very greatly assists in building up the size of the crest of the wave that follows. Finally, the upward movement of part of the air also adds to the height of the crest, whilst the downward moving air, by its additional pressure, increases the depth of the trough. By all these ways, the waves continue to grow larger and larger (Fig. 8).

The size of the waves that are produced in this way clearly depends on the strength of the wind, on the amount of turbulence and especially on the length of time for which the wind has played on each particular wave, for as we have just seen, as time goes on, the wind gradually builds up the size of the undulations.

.... grows and moves

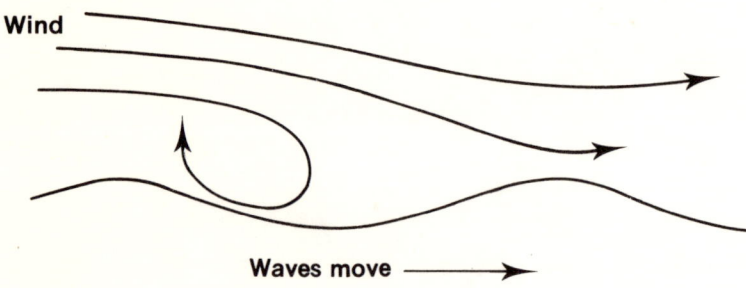

Wind

Waves move ⟶

Fig. 8 Waves become larger and larger

Wind and wave direction ⟶

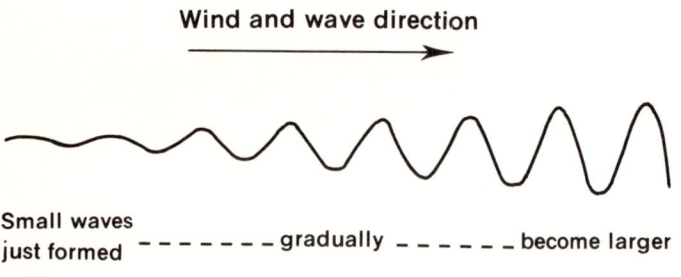

Small waves
just formed – – – – – gradually – – – – – become larger

Fig. 9 Wave-size partly depends on distance travelled

Length of fetch

If we go down-wind, we move into a place that has a longer length of fetch, for we are now farther from the land that lies to windward. So the waves will be larger (Fig. 9).

Alternatively, we may stay where we were at first, and the wind-direction may change. If the land to windward from the new direction is a different distance away, then the available length of fetch will alter and the size of the waves will also change. Naturally, too, the size of the waves depends upon the wind-speed.

All this is of first importance, not only to seamen who have to sail their vessels across these waves, but also to everyone who is concerned with any coast.

Supposing that most gales are of much the same speed, it is this matter of length of fetch that controls the maximum size of wave which a particular shore has to contend with, and this, of course, controls the severity of the forces that are producing erosion.

The map of the Irish Sea illustrates this point (Fig. 10). It is drawn to show the different lengths of fetch that are available for winds blowing from different directions on to the coast of south Lancashire. You will see that the maximum length is from the west, and is about 200 km. If the wind comes from the north-west the waves cannot have travelled for more than 115 km by the time they reach south Lancashire, because of the obstruction caused by the Isle of Man. Similarly from the south-west, they have only 80 km of sea available.

Thus the largest waves that reach this part of the coast must come from directly west, and even then they cannot have come from more than 200 km away.

This one fact is probably more important than anything else in controlling the features of this coast. A great deal of the Irish Sea coast consists either of sand dunes or boulder-clay cliffs and these would be eroded away very rapidly if

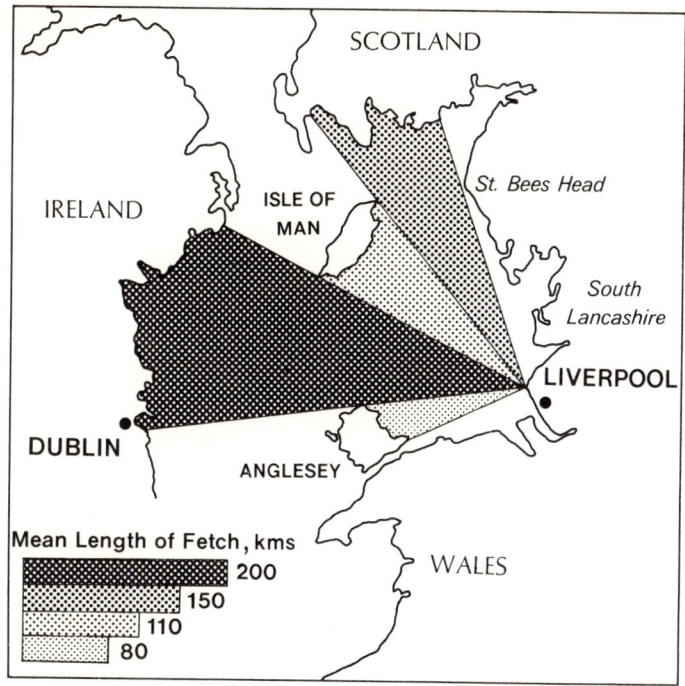

Fig. 10 Wave-approach to South Lancashire

of the Irish Sea, and consequently in these places we find high upstanding cliffs resulting from the erosion by these larger waves. The coast of the eastern side of Britain, both in Scotland and England, has an appearance which is intermediate in ruggedness between the Irish Sea coasts and those portions that are exposed to the Atlantic rollers. The available length of fetch in the North Sea is greater than in the case of the Irish Sea, but much less than for the Atlantic coasts.

It is these larger waves that make surf-bathing possible in suitable parts of Devon and Cornwall.

Waves on a small lake

You may easily observe the effect of length of fetch by visiting the lake in your local park. On a fairly breezy day, pay a visit to the nearest sheet of water, and you will see that at the side of the lake from which the wind is blowing the ripples are scarcely noticeable, and that as you walk round the lake, although the strength of the wind is not changing, you gradually have larger and larger ripples alongside you, until, when you reach the far end of the lake, you will find that relatively quite large waves are beating against the shore.

There is a practical point to learn here. If ever you are rowing on a lake, and a stiff breeze suddenly blows up and produces uncomfortably large waves, row into the wind so that you approach the windward shore. Not only will this be the most sheltered part of the lake, but also the waves will be quite small, even during a storm, because of the very short length of fetch.

There is just one more thing we should say before we leave this most important subject of wave size. Waves do not continue to grow and grow indefinitely, even with longer and longer length of fetch. There is a maximum height for a particular wind speed, even with unlimited

they had to suffer the pounding of really large waves. It is only because of the small size of the waves that these weak coastlines can survive.

It is well known that if you visit Devon or Cornwall you have the chance of seeing large waves. We even have a special name for them—Atlantic rollers. This part of the coasts, together with the west coast of Scotland, is in general very much more battered by the waves than are the coasts

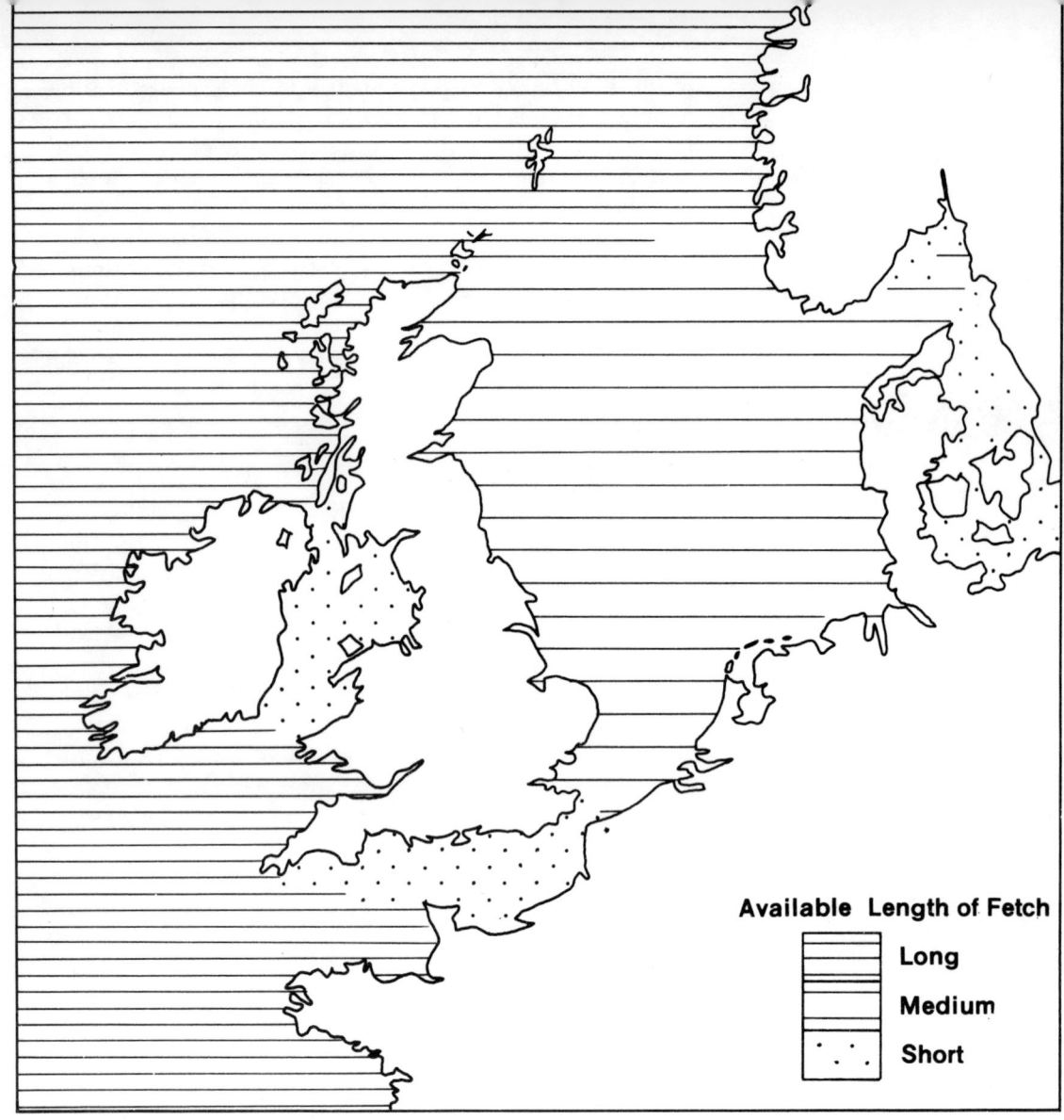

Fig. 11 Waves around the British Isles

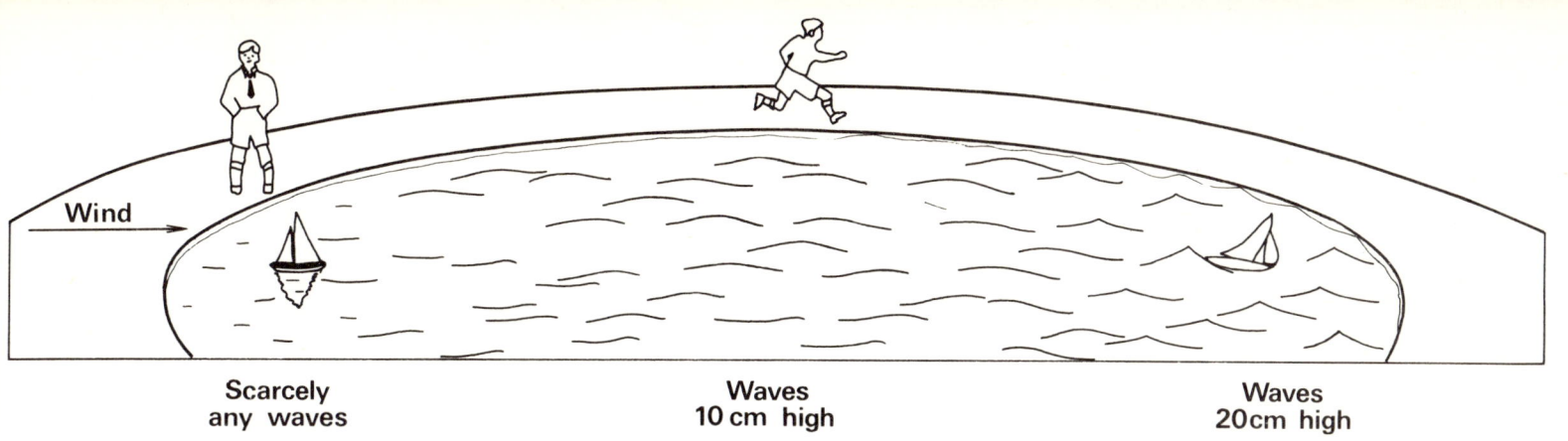

Wind

Scarcely
any waves

Waves
10 cm high

Waves
20cm high

Waves increase in height with longer length of fetch

Fig. 12 A practical experiment

Fig. 13 Ripples at the windward end of a pond

Fig. 14 Waves at the lee of a pond

length of fetch. It has been said that the maximum size measured in metres is about one-tenth the wind speed measured in kilometres per hour. Thus a wind of 30 k.p.h. cannot produce waves more than three metres high, however long the length of fetch may be.

Waves free-wheel

When waves have once been formed, they require very little energy to continue their movement. They are thus able to travel for many miles across the sea after the wind that generated them has ceased to blow. Waves of long wave-length decay more slowly than short ones, and it may quite often occur that a wave of, say, six metres amplitude will still be of some height when it has free-wheeled for even 1500 km. This explains why quite large waves reach open coasts when there may be little or no local wind. They have come from far away.

Such waves are technically known as free waves. When their amplitude has become fairly low, they are referred to as ground-swell or simply as swell.

Fig. 15 Atlantic rollers at Perranporth, Cornwall

Waves may even still approach when there is an offshore wind, which is trying to produce waves in the reverse direction. This is clearly shown in Fig. 15, which shows the beach at Perranporth on the north-west coast of Cornwall. The rollers are free-wheeling in from the west, whilst at the same time the offshore breeze is blowing the spray seawards from the breaking waves. Naturally the contrary wind lessens the size of the waves that already exist, and in time destroys them completely and starts to make its own waves.

The wave, not the water, moves forward

We have spoken about waves moving forward. Notice that the word is *waves* and not *water*. It is only the shape that moves across the surface of the sea, not the water itself. To get some idea of what this means, take a long length of cord lying in a straight line on the ground (see Fig. 16). Hold

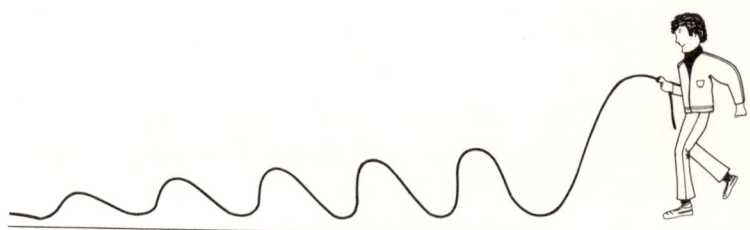

Fig. 16 Producing waves with a cord

one end in your hand and jerk your hand up and down as vigorously as you can. The vertical movement will travel along the cord as a sort of moving hump or wave. You realize that the wave travels along the cord, but the cord itself finishes where it started.

In the same way, there is very little forward motion of the water along the surface of the sea due to the waves. There is

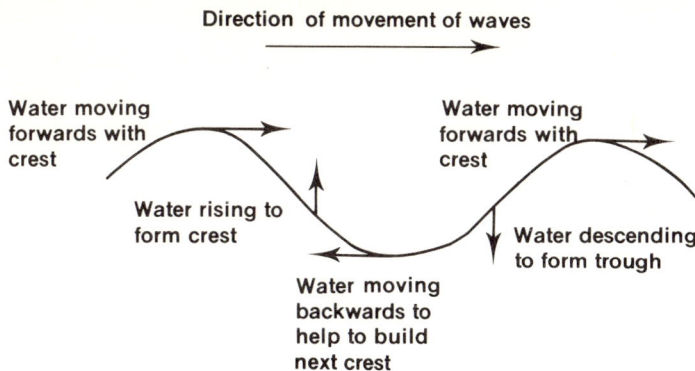

Water moving forwards with crest

Water moving forwards with crest

Water rising to form crest

Water descending to form trough

Water moving backwards to help to build next crest

Fig. 17 Water-particles move in circles

some movement, of course. The drag of the wind causes some water to drift along. But this is quite separate.

The individual particles of water move in upright circular paths in order to produce a wave (see Fig. 17). On the crest they are moving forwards with much the same speed as the crest itself. Behind the crest, they are moving downwards to make way for the next trough. In the trough, the particles are moving backwards to help the water forming the face of the next wave. There, the particles are moving upwards, to form the next crest.

If you imagine a wave passing by one particular observation-post, you will realize that, as one whole wave goes by, the water is first moving forwards in the crest, then downwards, then backwards, and then upwards. Then it moves forward again.

Watch a cork or gull floating on the water. As the waves pass, it bobs up and down with them, but does not travel along with them. It may gradually drift in some direction. Very often this may be in the direction of the wave movement because of the wind drag already mentioned, but sometimes it is sideways and sometimes even opposite to

the wave direction. This will be due to river or tidal currents and is quite independent of the waves.

When waves break

As geographers we are mainly concerned with the influence of the sea on the coasts. It is here, on the coastline itself, where the battle is fought between land and sea. Here certain types of wave build up beaches and so gradually increase the land-area, whilst other types remove the loose material and prepare the way towards cliff production. In the open sea waves are of great importance to seamen, but they hope never to be so near the shore as to have to consider, as we must, what happens when the waves come to the shallow water and eventually reach the water's edge.

When the waves reach shallow water, they break. It has been found that they do this when they reach water whose depth, if it were smooth water, would be about two-thirds their amplitude.

This happens mainly because, in shallow water, the full circular movement of the particles is hindered by friction on the bottom. As a result, the water in the crest of the wave continues forwards, but finds that there is insufficient water rising in front to support it (see Fig. 18). The crest is

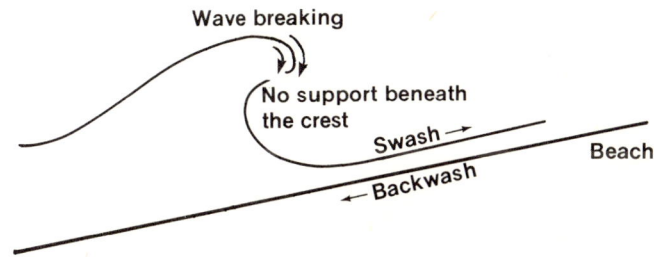

Wave breaking

No support beneath the crest

Swash →

← Backwash

Beach

Fig. 18 A wave breaks

now curling over a space only occupied by air. It is unsupported, and consequently collapses or breaks.

The movement is changed from a circular one and becomes a forward mass-movement of water. At the water's edge this is termed the swash. This is the advance of the individual wave from which you have to retreat hastily, if you are standing at the edge of the sea and do not wish to get your feet wet.

This advance upbeach is followed by the retreat of the water, as the trough of the wave follows the crest. This is called the backwash. Then in turn this is followed by the swash from the next wave, and so on.

Beach building

The plunge of the water, as the wave breaks, results in quite a fierce impact with the sand or shingle, that forms the floor of the sea just at this point. A considerable amount of the material is usually tossed up into suspension in the water. This moves forwards upbeach with the swash and is quite obvious in the water when you are bathing on a sandy shore. This water is quite brown with all the sand in it. Sometimes it is impossible to bathe comfortably on a pebble beach because of the hammer-blows you keep receiving on your legs from pebbles in the water. This movement of material with the swash builds up the surface of the beach.

If it is a sandy beach, the air-spaces between the grains will become filled with water when the first wave covers them, and so the backwash will drain downbeach on the surface of the sand, since it cannot hold any more water (see Fig. 19).

The vigour of the backwash is much less than the vigour of the swash, for the latter was forced upbeach by the strength of the approaching wave, whereas the backwash is little more than a glide back to the sea because of the

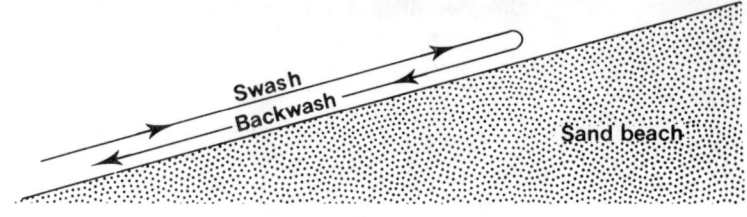

Swash and backwash both on surface of sand beach

Fig. 19 The water's edge on a sandy beach

downhill gradient of the beach.

As a result of this, much less sand and far fewer pebbles are taken downbeach than were brought up, so that the beach is continually built higher and higher by this action.

This is even more important with a shingle beach, for in this case the spaces between the individual pebbles are much greater than those between sand grains. The water between them is able to move so easily that it drains away between each wave (see Fig. 20). Every swash therefore finds itself flowing over pebbles with air-space between them, and as it comes to rest most of the water sinks into these spaces and drains back largely through the shingle-

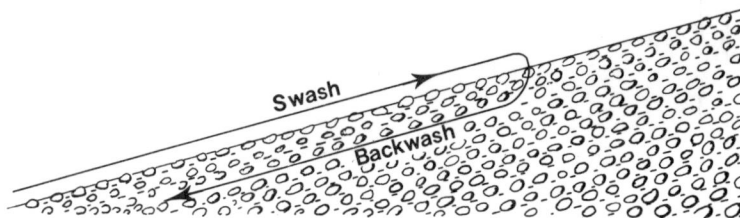

Swash on surface, and backwash amongst pebbles of shingle beach

Fig. 20 The water's edge on a shingle beach

mass, instead of on the surface. Consequently most of the pebbles that were brought up by the swash come to rest on the beach and only a small number are taken down again by the small proportion of the backwash that flows on the top surface of the beach.

Pebble beaches are much steeper than sand shores for this reason and of course a direct consequence of this is that the tide goes out a far shorter horizontal distance on pebble beaches.

This same fact also probably explains why sand and shingle are very often sorted out on those coasts where both occur. You generally find that the sand is farther down the beach than the shingle and this is because it is easier for the backwash to move the sand grains, even through the spaces between the pebbles.

Waves thus build up a beach whose slope is steeper if it is composed of pebbles than if it is made of sand.

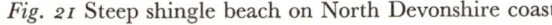
Fig. 21 Steep shingle beach on North Devonshire coast

Fig. 22 'Constructive' wave breaking

Constructive waves

All this depends upon each wave coming to the shore without interference from the others, and this occurs if there are something like six or seven waves per minute, which is very often the case. These are called constructive waves, since they build up the beach, and this frequency normally occurs if the wind has brought them from a considerable distance away.

Six or seven per minute means nine or ten seconds per wave, and this generally gives ample time for the backwash of one wave to get clear away before the swash of the following wave arrives. This action of each wave is thus completed without interference.

Destructive waves

Local winds, however, seem to produce waves of greater frequency, usually about twelve to fourteen per minute. And this also occurs if the waves reaching the shore have come from two sets of winds that have been superimposed on one another.

When there are as many as twelve to fourteen waves per

Fig. 23 'Destructive' wave breaking

Fig. 24 The sand almost covers a wreck

minute, there are only four or five seconds per wave. As a result the backwash of one wave meets the swash of the following wave, and spoils its forward movement. The two masses of water, travelling in opposite directions, collide head-on, and a great deal of the energy of the swash is used up in vertical movement of the water, instead of the usual horizontal forward movement. Naturally, therefore, the up-building effect of the approaching wave is considerably decreased, whilst the down-combing effect of the backwash continues unhindered.

These are called destructive waves and it is important to realize that the one and only difference between these and constructive waves is their frequency. Destructive waves are no more effective than constructive waves in their down-combing effect, but they have almost entirely lost their up-building power. Consequently there is a net loss of beach material from the coast.

Figs. 24 and 25 show two views of the same wreck on the south Lancashire shore taken one day after the other. A period of calm weather had built up the beach and nearly covered the wreck, as seen in the first photograph. But one night of storm with destructive waves had combed well over half a metre of sand off the whole beach.

This shows how much damage a single storm can do. In addition, the great confusion of waves had produced innumerable hollows in the sand. After a week or two of calm weather, the beach had been built up again by the constructive waves, and the wreck was once more almost completely buried.

It is important to realize that there are two ways of getting into debt. One is to increase your expenditure. The other is to decrease your earnings. The result is the same in each case—shortage of money! In the case of beach erosion, the shortage results from a decrease in accumulation, whilst the loss by down-combing remains more or less the same.

Fig. 25 After a storm, the wreck is exposed

2   Erosion

We are now ready to discuss the different types of coast that are produced not only by constructive and by destructive waves, but also by waves of varying size and direction. Naturally the result that is obtained does not depend upon the tools alone—the waves—but also upon the substance on which the tools are working. The kind of rock makes an important difference, not only the material—whether it is a relatively soft sandstone or a resistant granite—but also its structure. Cliffs in igneous rocks are not the same as those composed of sedimentary rocks, and the latter especially behave very differently according to the direction in which the strata slope.

The fact that the particular stretch of coast may be exposed to the full force of the approaching waves, or may be sheltered behind a protective headland, or may lie snugly in a narrow bay, also influences the result.

Abrasion platforms

Destructive waves quickly erode a sloping coast, and if the original land surface was as shown by the dotted line ABC in Fig. 26, and if the sea-level varies between positions 1 and 2 as the tide moves in or out, then the waves will cut a notch in the general slope and gradually advance over the more or less horizontal surface that they have produced. This is called a wave-cut bench or abrasion platform. It is marked BD in the diagram. The material that has been removed from the land may be deposited on the shoreface, as shown at AEB. Or it may be moved farther along the coast.

Naturally the waves are only able to erode the part of the cliff they can reach—the part that is below high-water level, or only a little way above it, within reach of storm waves.

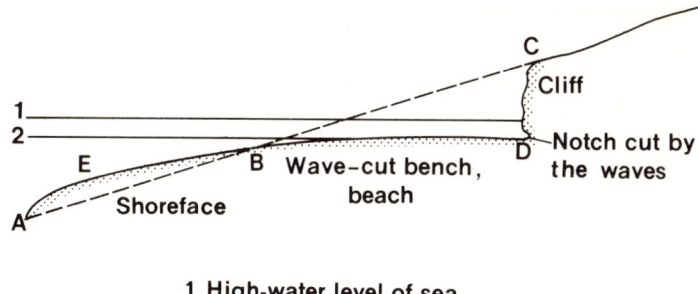

1 High-water level of sea

2 Low-water level

Fig. 26 Waves cut away the land

The main power of the waves lies in their ability to pick up pebbles from the beach and hurl them at the rock face of the cliff, so that it is continually pounded with a series of hammer blows. For a long time these may appear to have no effect, but all the time the individual blows are producing microscopic shatter cracks within the rock itself and eventually pieces of rock break off and fall into the sea. The waves are thus furnished with an additional supply of hammers. This process is known as abrasion.

When a notch has in this way undercut the foot of the cliff for a sufficient distance, the upper part is no longer supported and it collapses. The portion of any upright cliff face that is above the reach of the waves is always the result of collapse in this way, rather than of direct erosion.

Obviously the rapidity of the erosion, other things being equal, depends upon the length of time each day that the height of the tide allows the waves to beat against the cliff and also upon the size of these waves and how often they approach the coast concerned.

As the abrasion platform becomes wider and wider, shorter will be the periods of attack, for at most times the sea will now only reach the foot of the cliff at high tide, and even then the larger waves will break in the shallow water covering the abrasion platform. Gone is the time when the sea attacked the foot of the cliff for twenty-four hours every day.

Another important factor, too, is the rate at which the debris is removed after it has fallen from the cliffs (Fig. 27). So long as the cliff-face has this heap of broken rock at its foot, it is protected from further attack. Either destructive waves may remove the material to below low-water mark, or waves coming in on the skew may move it along the coastline. This process of **longshore drift** is described on page 41.

Types of cliff

The type of cliff that is produced depends upon the rock as well as upon the severity of the attack. Sand cliffs, for example, are never more than a metre or so in height, and then exist only for a day or two immediately after a storm. Sand is so easily washed away that it really never forms the coastline itself, except where erosion is very rare.

There are, however, many clay cliffs round our coasts but they generally suffer severe erosion and retreat rapidly.

Most of the lowland surface of Britain, except in the extreme south, is covered with a thick layer of boulder clay or other morainic material left by the ice sheets of the glacial period. This is the case in parts of north Norfolk, and at Mundesley, 11 km south-east of Cromer, there are clay cliffs over 35 m in height.

The rapid rate of erosion is clearly seen in Fig. 28, for some of the drills of corn, sown by machine only a few months before, had already been broken away and had fallen to the sea. When the machine treated this part of the field there must have been at least two metres more land on the seaward side, and this illustrates how quickly cliffs in

Fig. 27 Cliff rock-fall north of Newquay (Note the man standing on the left.)

Fig. 28 Erosion destroys the corn at Cromer

Fig. 29 Chalk cliffs near Weymouth

such soft material may be eroded.

Chalk is another material that is fairly vulnerable to wave-attack. Cliffs in chalk are usually upright as seen in Fig. 29 to the east of Weymouth, Dorset. The fallen material soon breaks up into small pieces when in the sea, and is also slightly soluble, so that very little loose material remains, and chalk beaches are normally quite narrow. The land surface in chalk country is gently rolling, with dry valleys. As there are no streams flowing along their floors, these valleys are not deepened as the coast advances inland. Consequently they remain unchanged, and are cut across by the coastline, producing a kind of hanging valley and the curious switchback effect of any chalk-land cliff-top walk.

When the upper part of a cliff is composed of material of a softer nature than the lower, the angle of slope of the cliff-face often changes at the junction. Flamborough Head,

Yorkshire, is a cliff 50 m in height and is shown in Fig. 30. It is composed of chalk below and a layer of boulder clay above. The chalk portion of the cliff is typical of this material—upstanding with a very narrow beach at its foot. The upper portion slopes backwards as the result of rain-wash down the surface of the clay. It shows some fine gullying where the rain has concentrated its flow, and this grooving has continued down into the chalk below. Here, therefore, in the case of chalk, we see both the action of waves and the action of rainwater.

In the case of chalk, the individual layers of rock do not determine the type of cliff produced. But in most sedimentary rocks the thickness of the individual strata, and especially their angle of tilt is very important, both in connection with rate of erosion and type of cliff produced. At Coombe Martin, in north Devon, Great and Little Hangman Hills (318 m and 212 m high) are composed of

Fig. 30 Boulder clay above chalk at Flamborough Head

Fig. 32 Backward-tilted strata produce vertical cliffs

Fig. 31 'Hog's-back' cliffs at Coombe Martin, North Devon

grit-stones (Middle Devonian, Hangman Grits) in layers which are tilted fairly steeply towards the south-west, as seen in the left-hand side of Fig. 31. As a result, the seaward face of the cliff slopes backwards roughly at right-angles to the layers, since the rock breaks off along the joints that lie in this direction. The surface behind the cliff-edge slopes down landwards with the dip of the strata. This produces a curious and distinctive profile, and it is known as a **hog's-back** cliff. Any rain which falls on this hill, if it is merely a metre from the cliff-edge, will drain landwards by a relatively long route to the sea.

The importance of attitude

This only occurs, however, if the joints are well developed so that the rock breaks very easily across the strata at these places. When the layers are tilted only slightly landwards, the cliff is very stable, and a fine, strong, almost vertical, wall of rock is formed, as at Kione y Ghoggan, on the south coast of the Isle of Man. This is shown in Fig. 32.

This effect may be illustrated if you try piling up a heap of books against a wall. You will find that the pile becomes very unsteady by the time you get it about one metre high, but if you insert a reasonably thick book just a little way under the outer edge of the bottom book, between it and the floor, you will find that the whole stack becomes quite stable because of the backward tilt you have given each layer (Fig. 33).

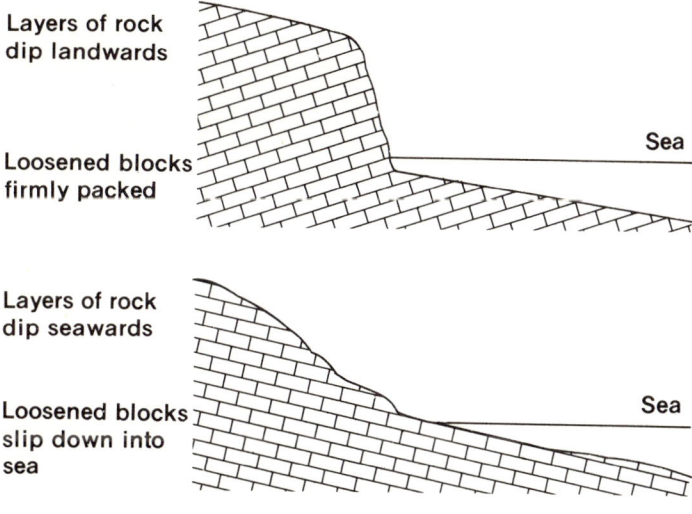

Fig. 33 Upright and sloping cliffs

The cliff at Kione y Ghoggan is over 60 m in height, and yet, within a few hundred metres, exactly the same rocks form a stretch of coast with scarcely any cliff at all. The two portions of coast both face south and are equally exposed to wave-attack. The only difference between the two is the **attitude** or tilt of the layers of rock. In the case of the portion shown in Fig. 34, the layers slope seawards. As a result, it is very easy for a block to slip away when it has

Fig. 34 The effect of strata sloping down to the sea

once been broken off the general rock by wave-action. It slides down the incline towards the sea. A number of detached blocks may be seen in the sea, both partially and completely covered by the water.

Clearly, it is necessary to consider many physical factors, as well as the actual kind of rock, when thinking of the kind of cliff that waves may be expected to produce.

Cliffs in igneous rocks

Igneous rocks, unlike sedimentary rocks, are not in layers. Consequently the strength of these formations mainly depends upon the spacing and the weakness of the jointing. Granite cliffs, such as those at Land's End (Fig. 35), very often possess many vertical joints, so that they have a tendency to produce upright columns, and form a **castellated** cliff. The stability of this type of cliff depends very

Fig. 35 Castellated granite cliffs of Land's End

Fig. 37 Stepped cliffs at Giant's Causeway

Fig. 36 Basalt at Giant's Causeway

much on the horizontal jointing. If these joints are tilted even slightly forwards, then the columns of rock standing on them are much less stable and the erosion of the cliff will be very much more rapid.

An extreme case of this vertical jointing is at Giant's Causeway, Northern Ireland, where the 'beach' consists of thousands of upright hexagonal (six-sided) columns of basalt, with exactly horizontal transverse joints (Figs. 36 and 37).

Basalt is an igneous rock, which poured out from cracks in the Earth's crust so hot that it was sufficiently fluid to spread in great sheets over the north-eastern portion of Ireland and form the Antrim plateau. After the liquid basalt had become solid, further cooling caused contraction and produced this special jointing. On the north coast the

26

sea has etched out a wave-cut platform of most unusual form. Towering behind the Causeway are magnificent cliffs consisting of several thick deposits of the dark grey basalt, mostly columnar, which form upright cliffs, with bands of fairly soft, red, rotted basalt, called laterite. These softer parts weather to form sloping portions to the cliff. The result is the stepped-back effect shown in Fig. 37, and the alternating grey and red colours, together with the bright green grass that grows on some parts of the laterite, produce a cliff that is one of the most remarkable to be seen anywhere.

Besides the general form of the cliff, depending mainly on the various factors that have been described above, the detail pattern of the erosion is interesting also. Just one example is illustrated—that of Carboniferous Limestone at Scarlet Point in the south of the Isle of Man (see Fig. 38). The individual layers of massive limestone, each about 30 cm thick, are separated by thin layers of mud, so that the division along the strata planes is particularly definite. When the waves reach the rock, this results in the production of the step-like pattern shown in the picture. This photo-

Fig. 38 Stepped cliffs in limestone

graph was taken at low tide. The sea is visible on the sky-line, and the foreground is the top surface of a layer of the rock, from which the waves have removed the upper stata so perfectly that there is not a single blemish on this perfectly smooth surface. The darker colour of the mud layer on the 'tread' of each step may easily be contrasted with the very much whiter colour of the limestone as seen on each 'riser'.

Inlets and caves

So far we have been thinking of the cliff-face just as an upright wall. However, the waves soon find any specially weak points in the rocks that they are attacking, and erode faster there than round about.

We have already emphasized that waves can only erode what they can reach. The upper part of a cliff over an easily eroded portion may or may not collapse when the underlying rock is removed by the sea.

The resulting caves often are not very large, and practically the whole depth of one at Port Erin can be seen in Fig. 39. It has been etched out of the cliff-face, not because of a particularly soft band of rock, but because a vein of dolerite, an igneous rock, which had come into position hot and molten, had baked and so severely cracked the Manx Grits on either side of it that they were easily eroded. Then the unsupported dyke fell away. Its bleached surface may be seen as the broad sloping rock on the right-hand side of the cave.

Near Spanish Head, on the south coast of the Isle of Man, there is a cave formed by waves that have removed the rock from between two faults (Fig. 40). These can be seen very clearly on the cliff-face, as they continue upwards along the lines of the two side walls of the cave. They splay outwards slightly as they rise up the cliff, and this has the effect of making the upper rock rather like the keystone of

Fig. 39 Cave at Port Erin, Isle of Man

an arch. It has become wedged, and thus, jammed tightly, it has not fallen. Only the rock that the waves reach has been eroded.

Occasionally the thickness of the roof over a cave is not very great and for a variety of reasons it may collapse at its inland end. This is sometimes described as being the result of the explosive power of air, trapped in the inland end of the cave, when the mouth is closed for a moment as a wave sweeps in. The air within the cave is compressed, and, so it is said, blows out a portion of the roof. Perhaps this sometimes happens, but equally well a simple roof-collapse may be the cause, or even the gradual downwash of rock by the movement of underground water. Many of these caves were in the past the natural haunts of smugglers, for they afford very secret access to sea and land. The opening at the inland end of the cave is known as a blow-hole or gloup (Fig. 41).

Fig. 40 Cave formed by erosion between two faults

Fig. 41 Back entrance to a cave at Flamborough Head

The action of compressed air in cliff or cave erosion is known as **hydraulic action**. An open joint contains air. When momentarily the wave covers the exposed end of the joint, it seals the air in, and, if the water enters the joint, the air is compressed suddenly. Such action may be very powerful and when it happens at the back of the block, it may even drive the block forwards and out from the cliff-face.

Arches

It is only one step further from a cave to an arch. If the waves erode a hole through a narrow promontory of rock without the upper portion falling in, we have an arch, as on Holy Island, Anglesey (Fig. 42). It is plain here that erosion has followed the vertical jointing of the rock and that, as with the cave at Kione y Ghoggan (Fig. 40), there is a wedge or keystone action that has prevented the complete collapse of the upper rock. Notice that at Kione y Ghoggan it was a pair of faults, whereas here it is a pair of joints.

It is generally only necessary for an arch to collapse for us to have an isolated portion of land standing upright on the beach, or in shallow water, like a small island. This is termed a **stack**, and since it is more connected with the plan of the coast, than with the vertical profile of cliffs, we shall discuss this feature in the next chapter.

Fig. 42 A keystone arch

3   Coastal forms

The fact that a cliff exists at all indicates that wave erosion is taking place there. So many coastlines are cliffs because of the rise of sea-level at the end of the Ice Ages, something like 25 000 years ago. A great deal of the ice, that had existed in the form of glaciers and ice sheets, melted and returned to the oceans as water. Estimates vary considerably, but it seems that this rise in sea-level was of the order of about 150 m.

Coasts of submergence

As the water rose, land was drowned. The British Isles, which had been joined to the Continent, were finally separated as the Straits of Dover came into existence. The southern half of the North Sea was flooded. Many other similar changes took place.

The waves beat vigorously on the lands which they had invaded, and on the new coasts which lay open to their attacks.

Fig. 44 Partly drowned mountains

This general drowning produced what is known as coasts of submergence, and the type that occurs depends entirely on the nature of the previous land-surface, that has now been drowned. If the land was a plain, then the coast will be one of fairly straight plan with gently sweeping broad curves as is shown in Fig. 43. If, on the other hand, the area was hilly, then the mountain summits will still remain exposed above the raised sea-level, but the lower parts of the valleys of the old rivers will have been drowned, forming a series of headlands and inlets (see Fig. 44).

Fig. 43 Partly drowned plain

Rias

In some parts of the world the pattern of the landforms before the drowning was one of rivers coming down to the sea roughly at right-angles to the old coast. There were ridges of hills and mountains between the rivers. When this kind of scenery is drowned, you obtain a series of headlands with narrow bays (Fig. 44). Generally the bays are branching, for the tributaries were drowned as well as the main rivers. This produces what we call **rias**.

When the grain of the land lay roughly at right-angles to the coast in this way, the drowning produced what is known as the **Atlantic type** of coastline. But in some areas the ridges of higher land lay roughly parallel to the coast. Then the partial drowning produced a series of islands with narrow waters and straits between them and the main coastline (Fig. 45). The islands lie in chains one after the other, close to the main coastline and parallel to it. This is typical of much of the coast of the Pacific Ocean, and is why this type is often known as a **Pacific Coast**. The same effect was produced also along the coast of Yugoslavia on the eastern side of the Adriatic Sea (Fig. 46) and another name for this type of coast, derived from the area, is **Dalmatian coast.**

The ria type of coast occurs in Pembrokeshire, Brittany and north-west Spain as well as Devon and Cornwall. Rias give sheltered waters and often make excellent harbours. (See Figs. 47 and 48.)

The characteristics of rias are rather what you would expect. Remember that they are the result of the partial drowning of ordinary river valleys (see Fig. 49). They are deepest in the middle, with shallow water at the sides. The water gradually becomes shallower also as you go up the ria from the sea, until eventually it merges imperceptibly with the present river that flows into it. You may easily produce the effect of rias by taking the Ordnance Survey map of almost any hilly district and pretending that the land is drowned up to a certain level. Fig. 50 shows what part of the coast near Towyn, Merionethshire, would become if it were drowned to a depth of 60 m.

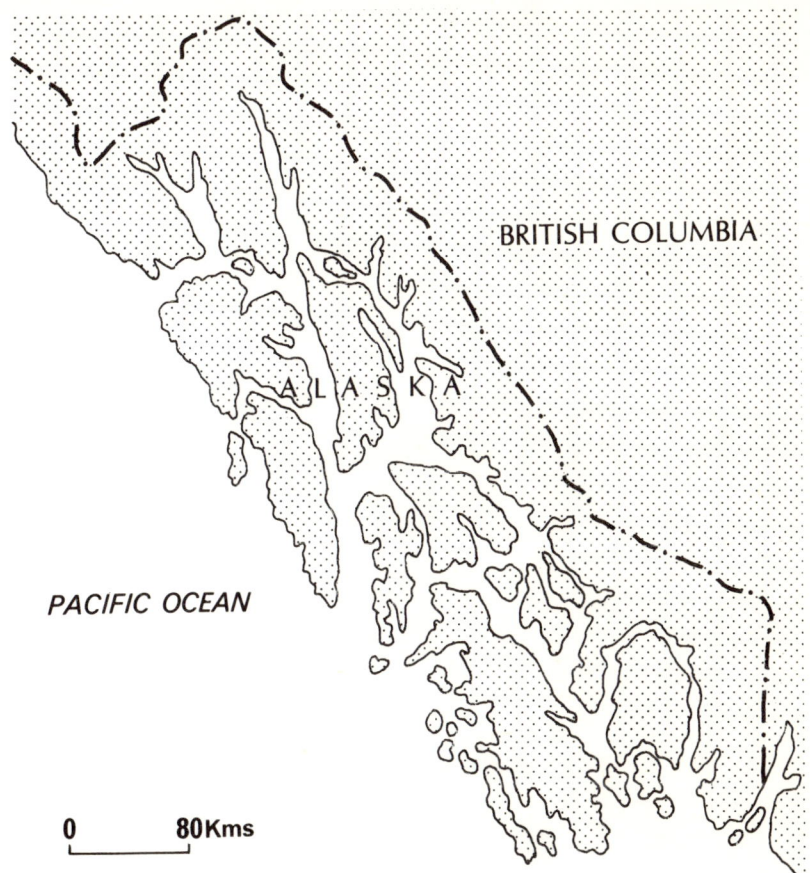

Fig. 45 Islands off the west coast of Alaska

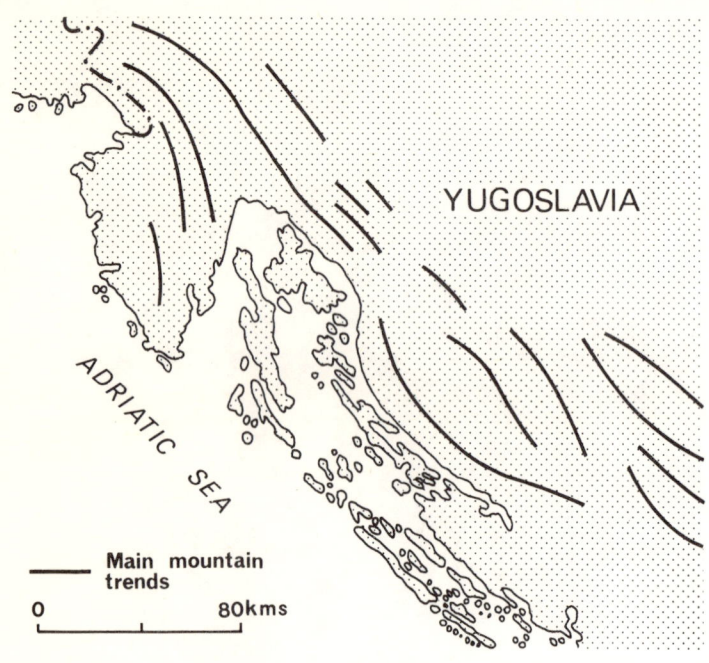

Fig. 46 Islands off the Yugoslav coast

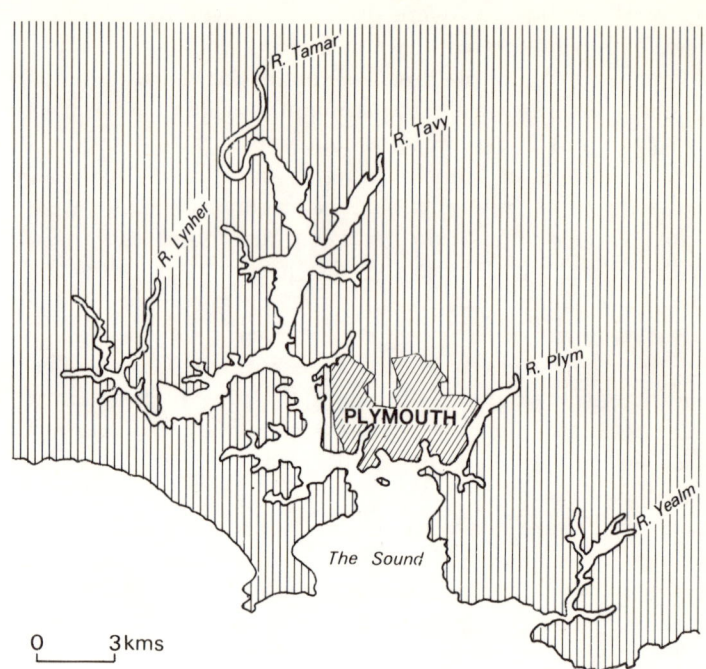

Fig. 48 Branched ria at Plymouth

Fig. 47 Fowey ria, Cornwall

32

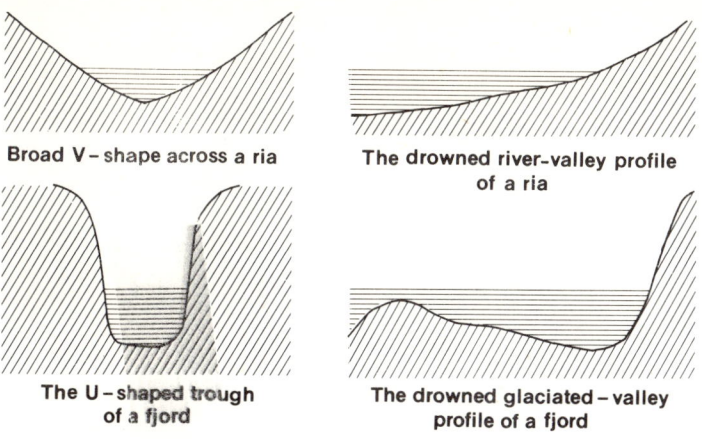

Broad **V** – shape across a ria

The drowned river-valley profile
of a ria

The **U** – shaped trough
of a fjord

The drowned glaciated – valley
profile of a fjord

Fig. 49 Differences between rias and fjords

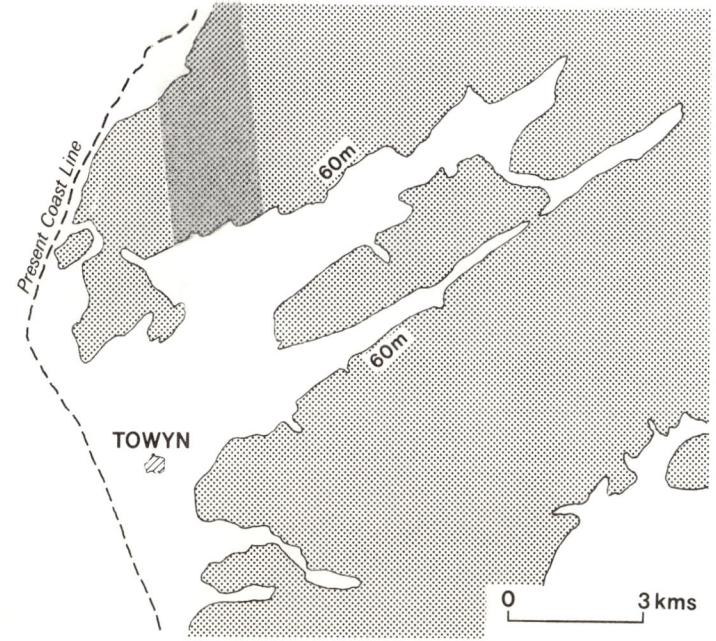

Present Coast Line

60m

60m

TOWYN

0   3 kms

Fig. 50 If the coast of mid-Wales were drowned 60 m!

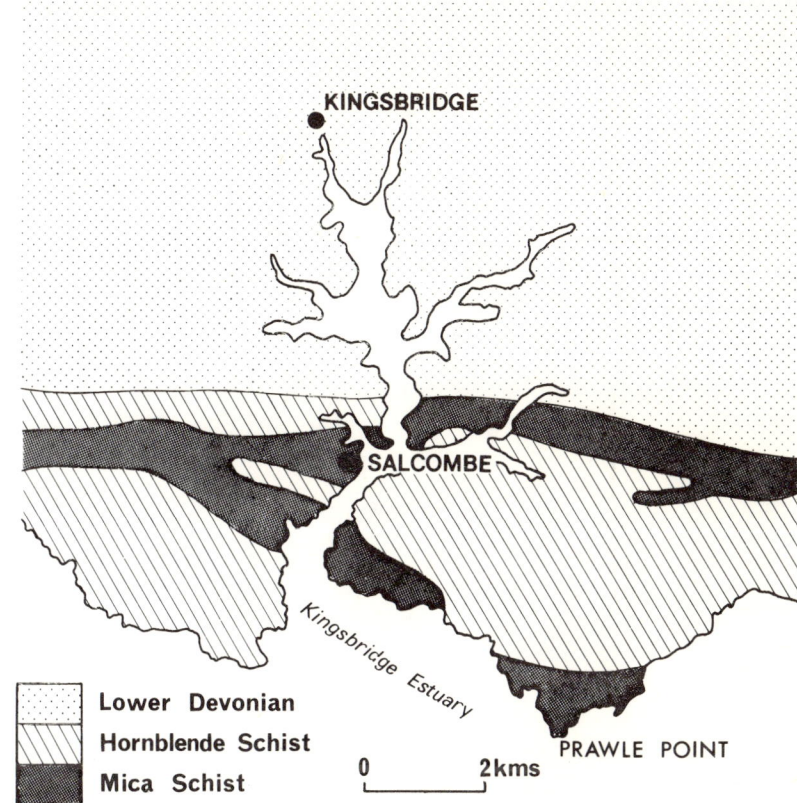

KINGSBRIDGE

SALCOMBE

Kingsbridge Estuary

PRAWLE POINT

Lower Devonian
Hornblende Schist
Mica Schist

0   2kms

Fig. 51 The Avon ria, Devon, ignores the geology

Two kinds of ria

Now part of the usual definition of a ria is that it shall be surrounded by fairly hilly country. On the map of the Avon ria (see Fig. 51), we have marked the different kinds of rock which occur. You will notice at once that the plan of the ria is not influenced by changes from one rock to another. In spite of the fact that the various rocks, the Devonian Grits, the Hornblende Schist, and Mica Schist, are quite different from one another with regard to their hardness and their resistance to erosion, nevertheless this change, from one rock to the other, does not show in any way in the shape of the ria. In other words, the pattern is not controlled by the geology. This is quite the common and regular behaviour for the rias that we have already mentioned.

There is another type of ria. It occurs especially in south-west Ireland (see Fig. 52). These rias also are famous for their beauty, and form the popular holiday area based on Killarney. They, too, are drowned river valleys. They are longer, straighter and wider than those of the south-west peninsula of England, and, contrary to the English ones, those in Ireland do result from the geological structure of the district. The shading on the map indicates that each of the peninsulas between these rias consists of a rock known as Old Red Sandstone, which belongs to the Devonian period. Most of the peninsulas are edged by a narrow strip of younger rock called Carboniferous Limestone, and this same limestone lies under the sea that has flooded the old valleys. This rock was formed on the sea-floor on top of the Old Red Sandstone, when that part of the Earth's crust was below water more than two hundred million years ago.

Since that time the area has been raised above sea-level, and puckered into a series of 'ridges' and 'hollows' which geologists call **folds**. The ridges are termed anticlines, and the hollows synclines.

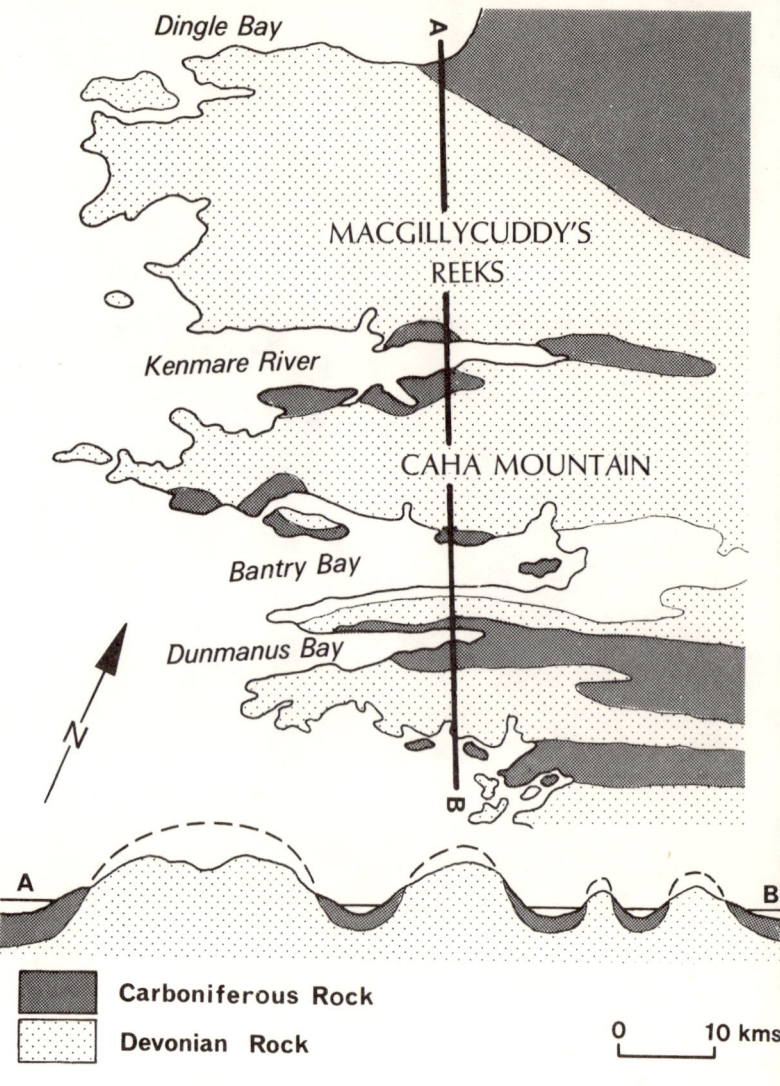

Carboniferous Rock

Devonian Rock

0   10 kms

Fig. 52 The ria coast of south-west Ireland

34

Rain has fallen on this land and washed away almost all the limestone from the ridges, leaving only the edging of it at each side and beneath the inlets. These synclines between the ridges were at first river valleys, but the sea has partly drowned them in the same way as it drowned the rias of South West England. These broad inlets of the ocean have, in this case, been formed as a direct result of their geological structure. They thus differ in their mode of origin from those of England and Brittany, although they are given the same name of ria.

Headland and bay

Naturally the headlands which project into the ocean between these inlets are particularly exposed to attack by waves, and so cliffs are formed at the ends of the peninsulas, as shown in Fig. 53. The material which is washed away has to go somewhere, and a good deal of it finds its way into the bays and forms bay-head beaches. You will nearly always find that where there are inlets you have beaches at the inner end. The headlands are, by contrast, nearly always fine upstanding cliffs, since they are exposed to the waves. So erosion occurs on those parts which project most into the sea, and building-up occurs in those parts which are most sheltered.

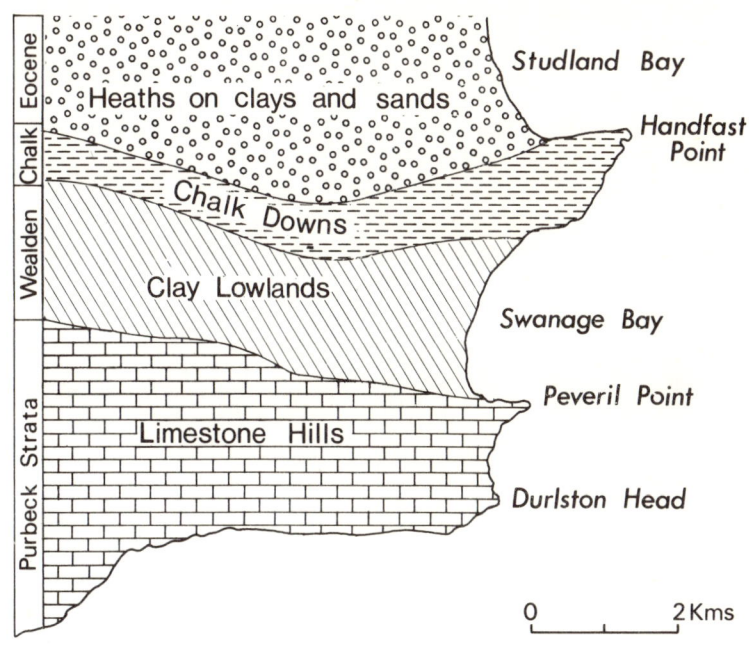

Fig. 54 Headlands in the harder rocks of Dorset

Fig. 53 Headlands attacked by the waves

The result is that gradually, as time passes, the coastline is straightened. The waves seem always to aim at producing a straight or gently curving coastline. They destroy headlands by eroding them, and bays by filling them. (See Fig. 54.)

Detailed wave-attack

Wave-attack takes a considerable length of time, and at first the waves erode where they most easily can, that is, in general, on the headlands. In detail, however, there is a good deal of variation as to where erosion takes place. The waves find out the weak spots in the rocks, and attack them. The resistant points are left standing, while the general coastline retreats landwards. The early result of wave-attack on a new coast is that it becomes less smooth in detailed plan than it was to start with. This is typical, for example, of parts of the south-west peninsula of England. This area is famous for its little bays or coves, sheltered between two headlands. It is the minute irregularity of the coastline, not only the rias themselves, that makes this part of the country so attractive.

This unequal shaping of the plan of the coast may be found in all kinds of stages. At Lulworth Cove, in Dorset (Fig. 55), the chalk downs are faced by a fairly thin, vertical layer of Portland Stone and various other rocks of Upper Jurassic age. Near the top of Fig. 56, on the extreme right,

Fig. 56 Lulworth Cove and Stair Hole, Dorset

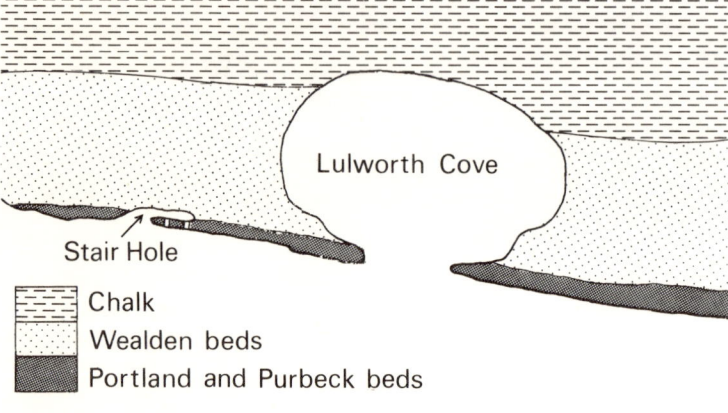

Lulworth Cove

Stair Hole

≡ Chalk
∴ Wealden beds
■ Portland and Purbeck beds

Fig. 55 Break through the resistant rocks in Dorset

just to the right of the buildings, is seen the gap in this hard bed, through which the sea has broken completely. Once they had cut a way through, the waves were able to erode sideways, as well as forwards, in the much softer Wealden Beds and Cretaceous Chalk. So the circular and almost landlocked bay of Lulworth Cove has been etched out.

Similar action is seen taking place at the foot of the same picture. This is Stair Hole. The ridge-like cliff on the extreme right is made of Portland Stone. Fig. 55 shows that it has been completely broken beyond the lower edge of the photograph, and there are also several arches cut through it by the waves, which are now busily eroding the beautifully folded rocks seen at the far end of the hole. This Lulworth crumple is famous with geologists all over the world, as an excellent example of sedimentary strata that have been so unequally lifted by earth-movements that the layers are now vertical (on the left), and with very sharp folding.

Only a remnant of the harder rock remains at Durdle Door, west of Lulworth Cove, and it is now linked to the mainland (Chalk) by a narrow neck of softer rocks. The Door itself is the arch that is seen at the nearer end of the hard Portland Stone in Fig. 57. The strata here are still practically upright, and this fact, together with the rapidly varying hardness from one (vertical) layer to the next, has resulted in this most fascinating stretch of coast, flanked on the landward side by the green grass-covered downlands of white chalk that forms the bulk of the cliff-line. The headland in the middle distance owes its existence, too, to the presence of low reefs of the same hard Portland Stone.

Isolated areas of harder rock, such as are often formed as the result of igneous intrusion, very often result in headlands, since they themselves are generally more resistant to wave-erosion than are the surrounding rocks, and also by their presence they protect the softer rocks immediately behind them. Many examples could be found to illustrate

Fig. 58 Headland of igneous rock at Criccieth, North Wales

Fig. 57 Durdle Door, west of Weymouth

this point, but the one chosen is Criccieth, North Wales (Fig. 58), where a hard plug of igneous rock forms the headland with steep cliffs on three sides. On this Criccieth Castle was built, with the town nestling on the landward side.

Stacks

In the case of Durdle Door, we saw an example in which the sea had broken away the harder rock on both sides and had worked round, so that the resistant Portland Stone is now only connected to the mainland by a very narrow neck of rock. Often this neck itself is completely removed, so that we are left with an upstanding, isolated rock in the middle of the beach. This is called a **stack**.

Fig. 59 The stacks at Bedruthan Steps

There are very fine examples of stacks at Bedruthan Steps, just north of Newquay, Cornwall (Fig. 59). They also occur at Tenby in South Wales and in many other places around the British coast and those of other countries.

They stand as reminders that they were once part of the mainland, and they give some measure of the minimum amount of erosion that has occurred. We realize that the waves have done much work in the past and that they will continue to erode in the same way in the future. Every land is being attacked by the sea around its borders, besides being attacked by the weather and rivers and so on over its whole surface.

Such irregularities as coves and stacks are recognized as being the sign of a youthful stage in the history of a particular coast—a stage when erosion has only just set in, or has recently been accelerated. Eventually the headlands are washed away beyond the landward limits even of the original bays. The whole coastline is straightened to one gently curving cliff-line. We see this process half completed at Ballintoy, Northern Ireland, with its broad, fairly sheltered beaches of sand and shingle, and widely spaced headlands.

Ultimately, however, so long as cliffs exist at all, we find something like the coast in the district of Seaton, Devon (Fig. 60), where a smooth gentle sweep of the coast ignores changes in rock resistance, and continues on, irrespective of whether the land be low or high. The coastline has passed its youthful stage, and has reached what is sometimes called maturity.

We have been discussing destruction. The subject has been coastal erosion. We must now pass on to a study of accumulation. We must find out what happens to the broken rocks that are washed away from the cliffs.

Fig. 60 Gently sweeping coast at Seaton, Devon

4   Beaches

We have seen how waves may result in either the up-building or the down-combing of the beach. The cliffs and other coastal forms that we have just been thinking about all result from the down-combing of the beach by the so-called destructive waves, for when the level of the beach has been lowered, deeper water is brought nearer to the actual coastline, larger waves break farther inland, and so the attack is closer to the coastline itself.

A low shore always encourages erosion. The one essential condition that must be fulfilled, therefore, in order to prevent coast erosion, is always a high level to the beach. The sea does not then often reach the foot of the cliff. On the occasions when it does, it is still only fairly shallow water, so that large waves break when they are some distance away, and spend their energy harmlessly (Fig. 61).

Wave refraction

As we have also already seen, the beach material, whether it be mud, sand or shingle, is moved about by the swash and backwash of each wave. So far we have only thought of the case when the waves arrive square-on to the coast. The physicist would call this direction normal to the coast, borrowing the word from its technical meaning when he is dealing with rays of light. The crests of the waves then lie parallel to the coast and approach along a path at right-angles to it.

However, since the direction of the wave movement is the same as the direction of the wind that produced it, and since winds blow, and coastlines lie, in all directions, quite clearly the waves will very often approach a coast on the skew, or obliquely, as shown in Fig. 62. When they approach shallower water, the rate at which the waves travel forward decreases, and so when we have the position AC, in which the end A is in shallow water but the end C is still fairly deep, we find that A travels forward the shorter distance to B in the same time that C takes to travel forward the greater distance to D. Consequently the lie of the crest of the wave is turned. This is called wave refraction, again borrowing the technical word from the subject of light. In this way the waves reach the waterline less obliquely.

The refraction is not complete, and the waves still arrive on the skew. This turning, and the fact that an angle still remains between the crests and the waterline, is well shown in Fig. 63, which was taken from the top of the cliffs at Lynton, north Devon. Where the crests of the breaking waves lie in deeper water, the photograph shows their angle on that day to have been something like sixty degrees with the coastline, but at the water's edge refraction has reduced it to about thirty degrees.

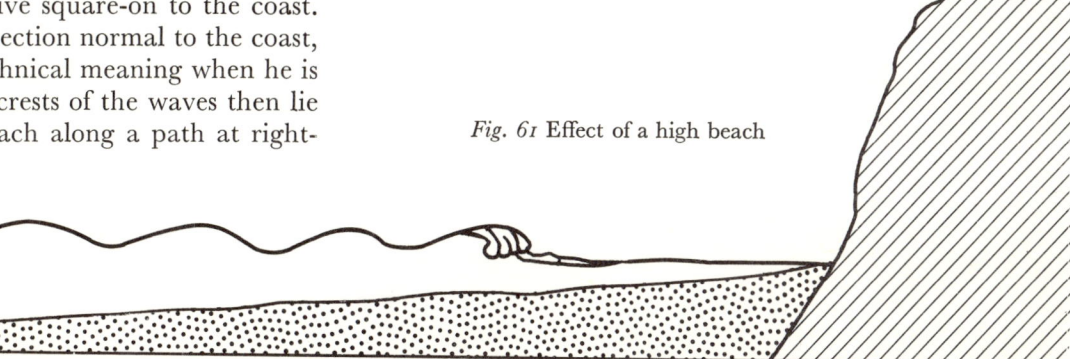

Fig. 61 Effect of a high beach

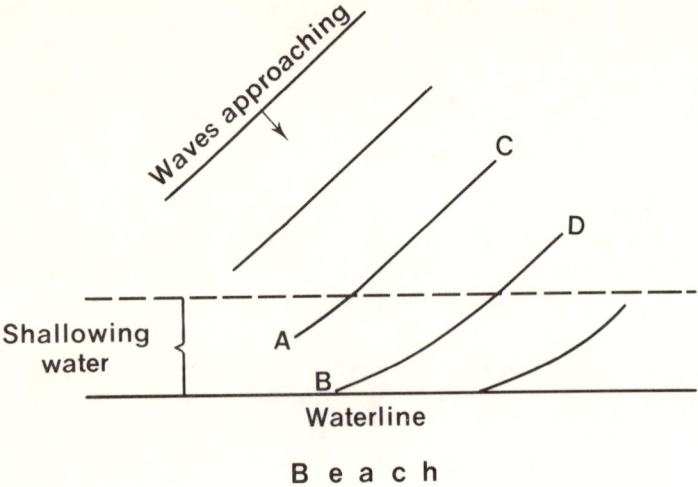

Fig. 62 Waves change direction as the water shallows

Fig. 63 Waves arriving at an angle to the coast

Longshore drift

Since this obliqueness is never completely wiped out, the direction of movement of the swash is still oblique also. This is illustrated in Fig. 64. If the waves approach as shown, the swash will move from A to B, and any pebbles or sand grains that were picked up when the wave broke will be moved in the same oblique direction.

The movement of the backwash is in the direction BC. It is not directly down the beach, but is a sort of reflection of the direction of approach. It is somewhat the same as a billiard-ball bouncing on the cushion of the table. The angles that AB and BC make with the waterline are not necessarily equal, for the steepness of the beach gradient influences the direction of the backwash.

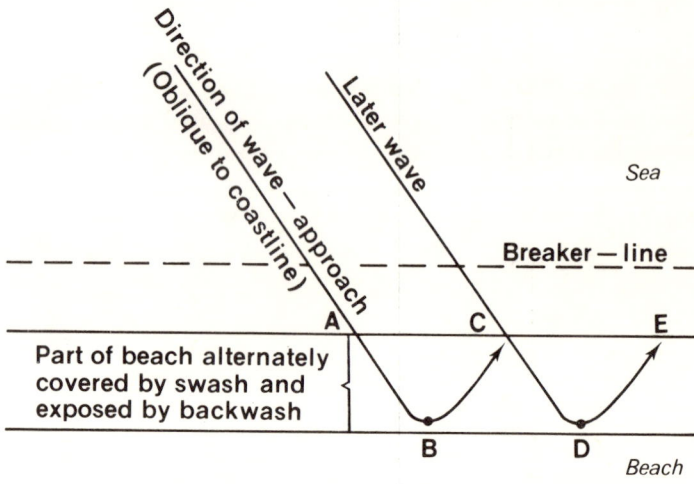

Fig. 64 Sand and pebbles are moved along the waterline

The whole result is that pebbles and sand that started somewhere near A finish their movement somewhere near C. Later on, they may be picked up by another wave, not necessarily the next one, from the point C and be taken by the path D to the point E. Thus the beach material is carried along the coast in the direction A to E. This is known as **longshore drift**, because it removes material from one place and deposits it in another. It is one of the most important factors in coastal change.

Cliff erosion by the pounding of the waves soon ceases if the rock that falls down is not removed. If, however, the fallen rock is carried away, the waves are able to continue their attack. It is longshore drift that is the main transporter. It occurs with both constructive and destructive waves, and thus goes on all the time, while the down-combing by destructive waves, which is the other method of removing loose debris, is only a feature of particular weather conditions.

One of the consequences of this longshore drift is that by erosion at one point and deposition at another, the tendency for coasts to become straightened out to face the oncoming waves, so far as possible, is greatly speeded up.

Beach control by groynes

Many towns, whose coast is suffering erosion, realize the importance of maintaining a high backshore, and also realize that the material of their beaches is moving along the coast in one direction or another. Very often these towns take steps to try to hold the beach material. They erect groynes across the beach.

Groynes are solid walls of wood or sometimes concrete. They are built from the coastline down to the low waterline, and they are intended to prevent the beach material from drifting along the coast. They very commonly show extremely well the direction in which the beach material is

drifting. You will generally observe that the shingle or sand is piled high against one side of the groyne, whilst on the other side the groyne stands quite a metre or more above the level of the beach (Fig. 65).

The difference in the height of the beach on the two sides of the groyne indicates the extent to which the groyne is preventing the material from moving. Very often those who have erected the groyne add more timber to raise its height when it is filled to the top on one side. This enables it to collect additional material.

Groynes are very successful in holding a beach, and also in raising the level where you require it. Like most things, they also have a disadvantage since, by holding the pebbles

Fig. 65 Shingle piles to the top of the groyne on its left-hand side

in one place, the groynes prevent them from going to another. Thus they starve the portion of the coast that is farther along.

This has happened over a very considerable length on the south coast, especially in the Brighton area. Here the beach material is moving towards the east. Consequently, when one town has erected groynes to hold pebbles on its own beach, the next town to the east finds itself starved of material, and so erects its own groynes. Then in turn the next town farther east has to do the same, and so on. There are literally hundreds of groynes along this stretch of coast.

One fact that should be emphasized about groynes is that they do not make beach material. They only control it. If, therefore, they accumulate it at one particular place, it is unavoidable that somewhere else is correspondingly starved. Before groynes are erected, it is always important to consider whether this starving may perhaps start off erosion in the starved area.

Sorting the beach

Suppose we now return to beaches which are in their natural condition, and have not been interfered with by man. A very interesting example of the result of the longshore drift is to be seen north of the Ribble estuary in Lancashire. The Ribble brings a considerable amount of mud, sand and shingle down from the Pennines. When it reaches the coast it enters an area in which the longshore drift is towards the north (Fig. 66).

As the river enters the sea, it first drops the portion of its load which is of larger size, that is, the pebbles. The direction of the waves forces all these pebbles on to the northern side of the estuary, so that Lytham St. Annes has a considerable amount of shingle on its beaches. There is not a single pebble to be found on the southern side of the estuary.

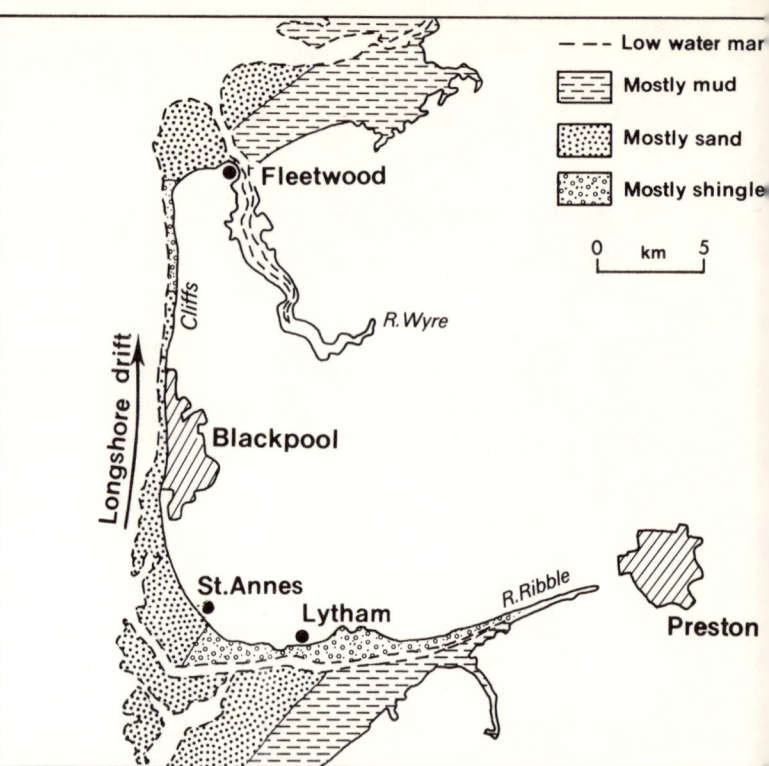

Fig. 66 Beaches north and south of Blackpool

The river is able to carry the sand, which it also brings down from the mountains, farther seawards. The longshore drift moves this sand northwards along the coast, round the corner to Blackpool. This is the reason why Blackpool has a sandy beach with practically no pebbles at all. At the northern end of Blackpool there are boulder-clay cliffs, which used to be eroded quite rapidly by the waves. So northwards of this point there are again pebbles on the beach. The sea-wall at Blackpool has been extended north to cover the whole length of these cliffs, and so no more erosion is taking place there. The beach farther north is now being starved of material, and so erosion is taking place near to Fleetwood.

Farther north still, round the corner again, to the east of Fleetwood, we find that there is a good deal of mud on the beaches, and it is quite probable that some of this mud is the finest material that is brought down by the river Ribble. It has been drifted northwards past Blackpool by the oblique waves, and has only managed to be deposited on the beach at this northern end of the stretch, where the quieter water gives it a chance to settle out.

Thus the mixed material that the river brought down to the sea is sorted out into shingle at one place, sand at the next, and mud beyond.

The map shows also that, when the coastline turns sharply eastwards at Fleetwood, the beach tends to continue straight on northwards. This very often happens. We could find an endless number of examples to illustrate this point, and you will be able to find many for yourselves by examining any large-scale maps that you possess.

Shingle spits

There is another very important fact that we must notice in this connection. So far we have been considering only those cases in which the material travels along the coast as part of the foreshore. When, however, shingle and sand moving in this way come to a sudden change in the direction of the coastline, it is very often the case that the drift continues on in the same line that it has been following and so springs away from the main beach and produces a spit.

This is another example of the tendency for coastlines to become straightened, or at least to assume a smooth outline. We have already dealt with the original occurrence of headlands of the more resistant rocks and their later destruction, producing a coastline with a straight or gently curving plan by means of erosion. But here we have the same result, either partly or completely achieved by the reverse process of deposition. In both instances, the final aim of the coastline is to face square-on to the largest and most frequent waves.

At Westward Ho! hills one hundred metres in height give place to the wide drowned ria of the river Taw. The cliffs to the south of Westward Ho! are being eroded by waves, which generally approach from a few degrees south of west, and thus the loose material that results from the erosion is moved along the coast past Westward Ho! and then tries to bridge the gap formed by the ria. The result is that a shingle ridge about 2 km in length has been formed. It is entirely natural, and has not been assisted in any way by man. On the landward side, in the quiet waters that have resulted from the growth of the ridge, mud has settled on the estuary floor, and grass has grown on the area so that it is now reclaimed land.

Similar ridges are to be found across several of the estuaries along the coast of Cardigan Bay, and one of these almost blocks the Dovey estuary (Figs. 67 and 68). This time the estuary is bounded by mountains to north and south. A shingle ridge has built itself across from the southern side. Again the direction of longshore drift is from south to north. The ridge has not succeeded in bridging the estuary entirely, since when the channel

Fig. 67 Shingle bars the Dovey estuary, Cardigan Bay

between its northern tip and Aberdovey becomes sufficiently narrow. the tidal scour of the sea, as it fills the remaining part of the estuary and empties it twice a day, together with the river current, is sufficient to wash away any pebbles that may tend to accumulate across it. As in the previous case, salt marshes have accumulated on the landward side of the ridge, and have now largely become reclaimed land. Man has assisted this with some artificial embankments and drainage channels.

A tombolo

One more example must be mentioned. The south coast from about a mile east of Lyme Regis to Portland Bill consists of a series of smooth, very gentle curves, as each portion tries to face a direction that is not very far from SSW. Most of the coast is experiencing erosion in fairly soft rocks. Every few kilometres the waves find that it is

impossible to maintain the ideal direction, and the coast steps back a little.

The cliffs at West Bay, Bridport, are, however, very high and very easily eroded. These have provided a plentiful supply of pebbles with which to continue the lie of the coast when, at Abbotsbury, the line falls away a little. The great shingle ridge of Chesil Bank then continues the general sweep, with a space, The Fleet, between itself and the mainland. Eventually it joins itself on to the Isle of Portland.

A shingle ridge that links an island to the mainland in this way is called a tombolo.

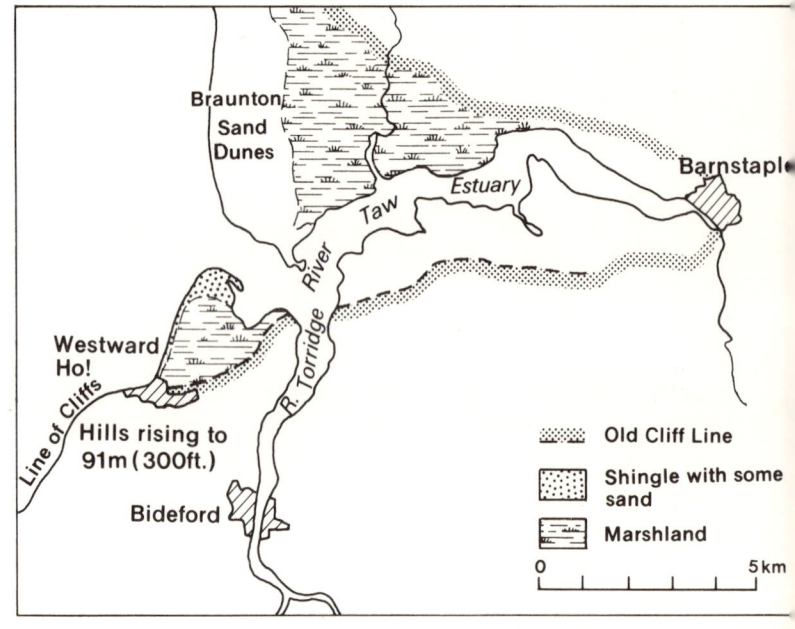

Fig. 68 The Dovey estuary

44

Section Two:

The Work of Rivers

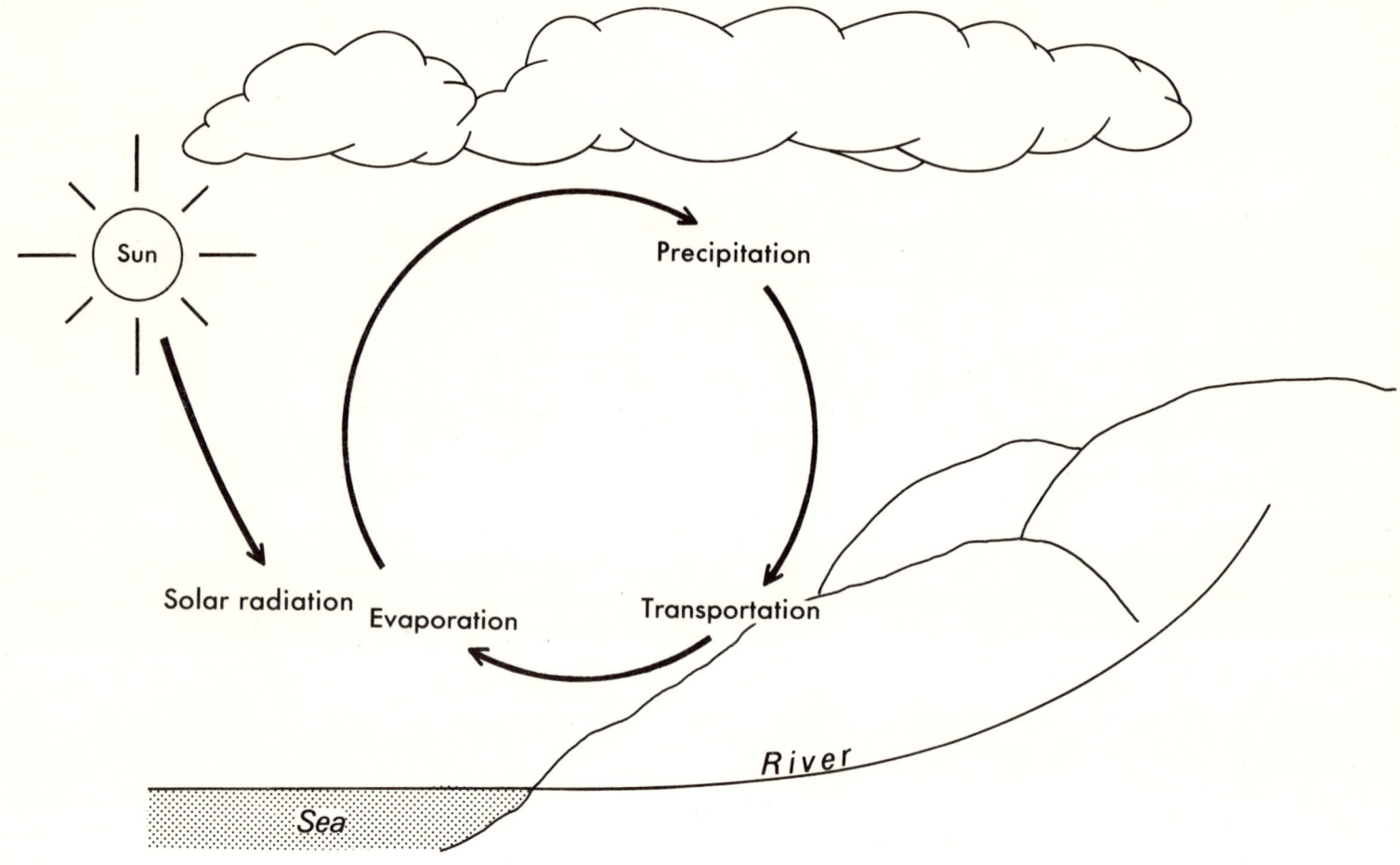

Fig. 69 Simplified water cycle

46

5　The water cycle

Water is probably one of the most remarkable substances on the Earth. We know how simple it is from the chemical point of view with its formula H_2O. It is the only substance we commonly see and use in the three states, solid, liquid and gas, and which has three separate names—ice, water and steam. Much more than half the weight of most plants and animals is water. No plant or animal can exist without it. Our whole life depends upon it.

Besides the oceans, there is the water frozen in ice sheets and glaciers, the water in lakes and rivers, and within the ground and in living plants and animals. How much all this is, no one can even pretend to estimate.

The water goes round and round

The water is constantly moving round through a series of processes which we refer to as the **water cycle.**

The sunshine beats down on the oceans as well as on the land (Fig. 69), and the warmth gradually evaporates some of the surface water. The water vapour so produced is a true gas, is completely invisible, and is perfectly dry. Only liquid water is wet. The vapour tends to rise. It becomes part of the air, and moves along with it as wind. In time it may pass over to a land area, where it may become a cloud. The microscopic particles of water or ice scarcely fall through the air at all, but when they become larger they descend to the ground as rain, hail, sleet or snow. For simplicity, we will suppose that if it comes down as ice, it soon melts.

Now this water has the choice of three possible routes before it (Fig. 70). Part of it will, in any case, be re-vaporized and return to the atmosphere in that way. We all know that after a heavy shower of rain a good deal of water runs down the grids in the gutters of our roads, but we also know that the roadway is left still wet. Nevertheless, half an hour or so after the rainfall has stopped, the road is once again perfectly dry. The final thin film of water which covered the ground has disappeared in the form of water vapour, completely invisible in the air.

The remainder of the rain will either stay on the surface of the ground and move downhill, as surface run-off, and soon form runnels, streams and rivers, or it may soak into the ground and become **underground water.**

The underground water has again two possible paths offered to it. It may remain what is called soil-water—the water between the individual grains of the loose soil of the surface—and some of it may be absorbed by the roots of plants growing there. In that case, the water will move up the stem of the plant to the leaves, and eventually most of it will be returned to the atmosphere once again by evaporation. Botanists call this process **transpiration.** Much more water is returned to the atmosphere direct in this way than we generally realize.

The remaining part of the water which is underground will soak through the spaces in the ground, and the way in which it does this will be discussed later (pp. 56–62). In time it will once more return to the surface, either in the form of a seepage or in more definite form as a spring. It then finds its way into rivers. Like the surface run-off, it too will eventually return to the sea.

This is the water cycle. The circuit is complete. We started in the oceans, and we have finished there.

In different climates, different proportions of the water which falls to the ground take the three different paths. In a very hot, dry climate, a great deal of the rain returns direct to the atmosphere as vapour. In fact, in some very hot desert areas, it occasionally happens that one can see rain falling from the rare cloud and actually being re-vaporized in the air before it ever reaches the ground at all—an extremely tantalizing sight for the few inhabitants who live below, and who are very much in need of water.

We are concerned in this section with that part of the water cycle from the moment when the rain reaches the ground to the time when the water arrives back in the ocean, whether it remains on the surface the whole way or whether it sinks below and travels underground for part of the journey.

As it runs over or through the land to the sea, it is able to remove considerable quantities of the rocks over which it passes. It carves valleys. It eventually reduces even mountains to the state of lowland plains. And with the material it has moved, it makes fresh land.

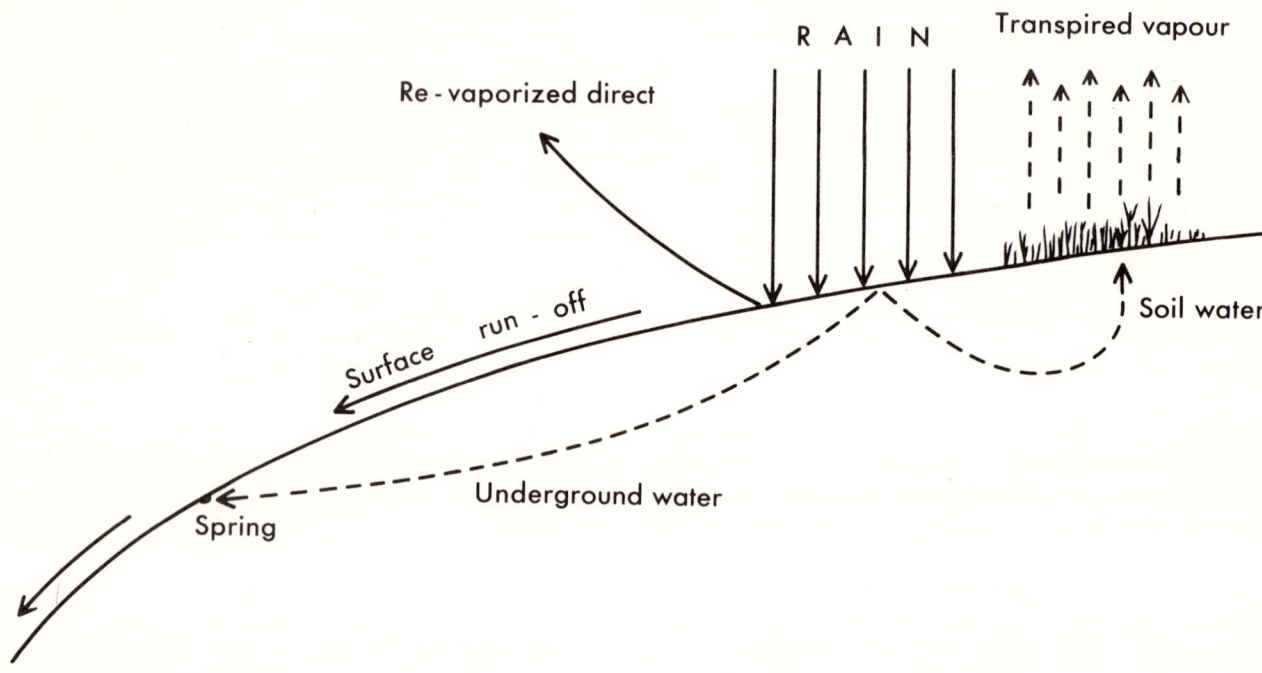

Fig. 70 After the rain has fallen

48

6   Weathering

Before rivers can wash rock down to the sea, it must be broken into pieces of suitable size. This break-up of the surface of the solid mountain is what we generally call **weathering**. It must be distinguished from **erosion**, which will be dealt with on pp. 63 ff. If the break-up occurs because of the mere presence of air, water or ice, we call it weathering. But if it occurs because of their movement, then we term it erosion. Moving air becomes wind, moving water becomes a stream, moving ice a glacier.

Exfoliation

In a dry climate with clear skies, the difference between day and night temperatures is considerable and this results in a type of weathering that is known as **exfoliation**.

The high day temperature warms the exposed rocks and as a result they expand. At night there is rapid cooling. The surface rocks shrink more rapidly than the underlying rock a few centimetres deep. The skin becomes too tight and it cracks. Consequently layers of rock peel off, rather like the layers of an onion, and the mountain eventually becomes rounded and dome-shaped, as is shown in the photograph of the Sugar Loaf mountain (Fig. 71). This is one of a number of similar peaks near Rio de Janeiro. Most of them are made of gneiss, but granite often weathers into the same shape, for this effect particularly occurs with igneous rocks that have very few joints and no strata or layers. As a result, these rocks can break equally easily in any direction. Individual granite blocks often show the same effect, as is seen in Fig. 72.

Fig. 71 Sugar Loaf Mountain, Rio de Janeiro *(Aerofilms Ltd.)*

Fig. 72 Granite blocks in Cornwall

Sometimes the joints in the rock are sufficiently close to one another for the pieces to become quite small ones. Fig. 74 shows Manx Slates on Spanish Head, Isle of Man, where the weathering has broken the rock down into almost pencil-like shapes.

When a large number of boulders are broken away in this manner, they sometimes fall on to fairly level ground and form a spread of boulders known as **felsenmeer**. This is seen in Fig. 75 in Snowdonia. Boulder-spreads of this type are quite common in mountainous districts.

Quite clearly, if this production of boulders occurs on the side of a slope, the individual rocks will fall downwards due to the action of gravity. In this way great heaps of debris are formed on the mountain sides. They are known as **screes**. Screes almost choke many valleys, as, for example, in Honister Pass north of Scafell (Fig. 76), and the detail of the toe of such a scree is shown in Fig. 77, which is at the top of Grisedale Hause, south of Helvellyn.

Freeze-thaw

Water is, however, most often the more active weathering agent. It works in two main ways: either by mechanical disintegration or by means of chemical changes.

When water freezes and turns to ice it expands by about one-twelfth of its volume. If the water lies in a crack or joint in the rock, or lies between individual grains, then the space between these has to enlarge. The portions of the rock on either side will be forced apart a little. The crack, or the pore space, will be widened. After the water has thawed, more water comes into the now slightly larger space. Next time it freezes, there will be a greater quantity of water present and more expansion will take place. Thus with each freeze and thaw, the crack or the space between the grains will become larger. Fig. 73 shows a joint widened in this way on the surface of rock in Glen Orchy, Argyllshire. Eventually a great block will be broken off.

Fig. 73 Water, turning to ice, widens a joint

Fig. 74 Intense freeze-thaw action

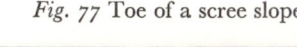

Fig. 76 Screes almost choke a glaciated valley

Fig. 75 A spread of broken rock

Fig. 77 Toe of a scree slope

Chemical weathering

The second way in which water can break down solid rock results from the chemicals it contains in solution. As rain falls from the clouds to the ground, it picks up a certain amount of carbon dioxide from the atmosphere and becomes a weak solution of carbonic acid. Because this acid can attack limestone or chalk, these rocks are particularly liable to what is often called **solution weathering**. **Chemical weathering** would be a better phrase, because the first thing that happens is a chemical change and then solution follows.

Limestone will not dissolve in water. But the acid in the water combines with the limestone to change the carbonate of lime into bicarbonate of lime. This bicarbonate then dissolves in water. The rock is slowly corroded away chemically, and where most rain lies most weathering of this type occurs.

Limestone itself is a rock which does not allow water to penetrate except by way of the joints, which appear like cracks in the rock every 30 cm or so. As most of the rainwater flows away underground through these joints, so their sides are slowly corroded by the chemical action. The joints therefore become wider by the removal of rock. A good example in a fairly early stage is to be seen on one of the limestone hills south of Kendal (Fig. 78), and in a more advanced stage on the side of Ingleborough near to Alum Pot, where the joints have been much more widened and the corners rounded off by the corrosion (Fig. 79). This type of surface is very characteristic of limestone country, and the features are known as grikes and clints.

Some other rocks are even more susceptible to chemical weathering than limestone. Granite is one of them. Fig. 80 is granite near Paimpol, Brittany. Grooves and all kinds of remarkable shapes have been produced. The locals call this one the tortoise rock. Quite probably much of this type of

Fig. 78 Widened joints in limestone

Fig. 79 Grikes and clints on Ingleborough

weathering occurred when the rock was covered by soil and the flutings mark the routes taken by ground-water. This weathering has been done by the direct chemical action of water itself, and not by the acids which it contains.

The mineral attacked is the felspar, which is one of the components of granite. Felspar will combine with water to produce a fine powder-clay known as kaolin. The volume of this clay is very much greater than the volume of the felspar from which it was formed. This expansion during the chemical change naturally pushes apart the remaining components of the granite. These are quartz with some mica.

Again, most of the action takes place where there is most water. As the corner of a block has three surfaces, the top and two sides, exposed to the water, greatest corrosion takes place there. This rounded-corner pattern is typical of granite country and it is sometimes difficult to distinguish between exfoliation and corrosion forms (compare Figs. 72 and 80).

Granite tors such as are seen on Dartmoor owe their origin to chemical weathering of this type which occurred when the whole mass was underground. The general surface of the land round about has been lowered since the rotting, leaving upstanding monuments of past disintegration.

Rainwater, soaking through the soil on which it has fallen, very often picks up organic acids from the humus in the soil. These organic acids are able to attack chemically a number of types of rock. This is one of the principal ways in which rock lying under a layer of soil is broken up into smaller pieces and so eventually becomes itself part of the soil. In Fig. 81 we see the disintegration of millstone-grit sandstone in Derbyshire due to filtering through the peat that lies on the surface.

Fig. 80 The effect of water on granite

Fig. 81 Rock changes to soil

Erosion by wind

Erosion by moving air is closely related to weathering and must be mentioned there. When wind blows over dry ground that is covered by sharp sand, it very often happens that the grit may be blown into the air and thrown vigorously by the wind at the surfaces of nearby rocks. There it acts very much like sand-paper, and gradually wears away the surfaces it comes into contact with. Fig. 82 is at Brimham, just north-west of Ripon in Yorkshire.

Since breezes are more frequent than storms, and since consequently the grit is raised to a small, more often than to a great, height, more erosion takes place at the bottom than higher up. In this way undercutting is produced. It so happens that in some particular cases the remaining column of rock is beneath the centre of gravity of the whole mass, and consequently, although it probably weighs something like a hundred tonnes, it has not yet toppled. The different amounts of erosion that have occurred at different heights may mark relatively soft layers of rock or may indicate particular levels to which the sandy grit is apt to be lifted. Fig. 83 shows another unusual formation in the same area.

Mass movement

After solid rocks of the mountains have been broken up in these various ways, there is very often considerable movement before streams start to take charge of the material. If the area is sloping, there is a general downhill drift of small particles aided by rainwater which seeps amongst the material itself. This is known as **soil-creep**.

There is also the process known as **solifluction**. This occurs especially in areas subject to freezing. If the ground composed of broken material has frozen solid for a depth of 30 cm or more, and then later the top few centimetres

Fig. 82 Wind erosion (*G. R. P. Lawrence*)

Fig. 83 Brimham Rocks, North Yorkshire (*Mrs. C. M. Lawrence*)

have thawed out, we have an interesting set of conditions. The ground is no longer porous and water cannot drain away through it because of the ice that occupies the pore and joint spaces below. The top few centimetres become water-logged and almost a stiff mud. This is lying on a layer of ice and frozen soil, and consequently the top layer of the whole hillside glides downhill. This movement is, of course, too slow to be visible to the naked eye. As it does so, the material may meet large boulders or projecting rocks and more or less flow around them. Some parts of the surface overtake others, and the ground becomes hummocky and uneven. This is shown in Fig. 84, which was taken among the mountains near Finse in central Norway. Solifluction was very important in Britain just after the ice ages, but is now important only at heights above about 700 m.

You all know how unpleasant it is to play games such as hockey and football on ground which has just partly thawed out after being frozen. There is the layer of slush on top of the still-frozen sub-soil. That is the condition which exists when solifluction takes place, but, of course, for the flow to occur it must be on a slope.

Fig. 84 Solifluction hummocks on the hillside

7   Underground water

We have already described how a portion of the rain, which falls on the ground, soaks into it and travels underground until it reappears later on as a spring somewhere on the side of the hill. Rock may be either permeable or impermeable. A permeable rock is one which allows water to pass through it. An impermeable one does not.

Permeable, porous, pervious

A permeable rock may be so in either of two ways. It may be porous or pervious. It is porous if the water is able to filter through by way of the pores between the individual grains of which the rock is made. This is possible whenever the rock is composed of separate grains that are only partially cemented together, so that there are continuous gaps between them through which the water may pass. This is common with sandstones and similar types of rock.

A rock may be non-porous but still let water through it. In this case it is said to be pervious. A pervious rock allows water to pass through because of the fact that it contains joints that are not water-tight. Limestone is a very good example of a rock which contains no pores, but which does possess a large number of joints. These are generally wide enough cracks to permit water to flow.

Springs

As the water sinks into the hill, whether it be by way of the pores or the joints, it is naturally subject to gravitation and moves downwards. Eventually it is likely to reach a layer of rock through which it cannot pass. It will then ride on the top of this rock, through the sponge, as we might call it, of the upper rock, in a downhill direction if the junction between the two rocks is sloping.

Sooner or later the junction will come out on the hillside, and there the underground water will reappear as a spring. It very often happens that we find a line of springs along the outcrop of the junction of permeable and impermeable rocks, a fact which is of great assistance to geologists, when they are trying to find the boundary between two types of rock.

The water-table

The spaces, whether they be joints or pores, may be filled completely with water after heavy rain. In that case the rock is said to be saturated. This is generally what happens with the lower portion of the rock above the impermeable layer. This is shown in Fig. 85.

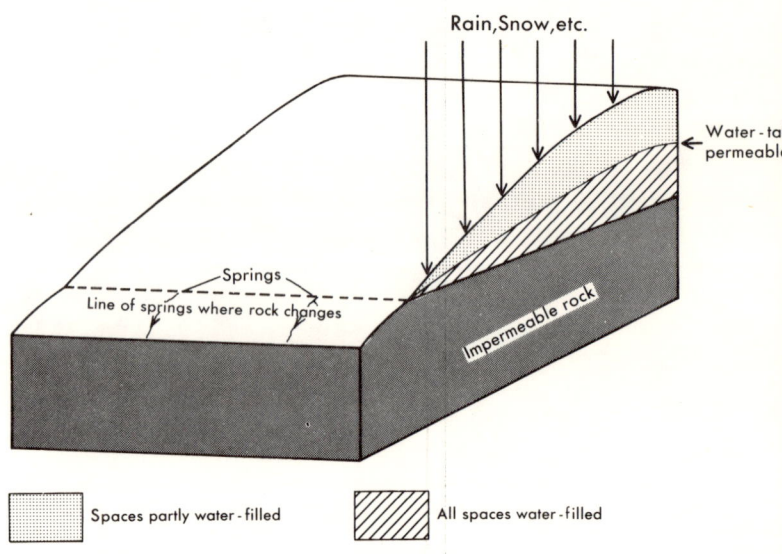

Fig. 85 Water-table and springs

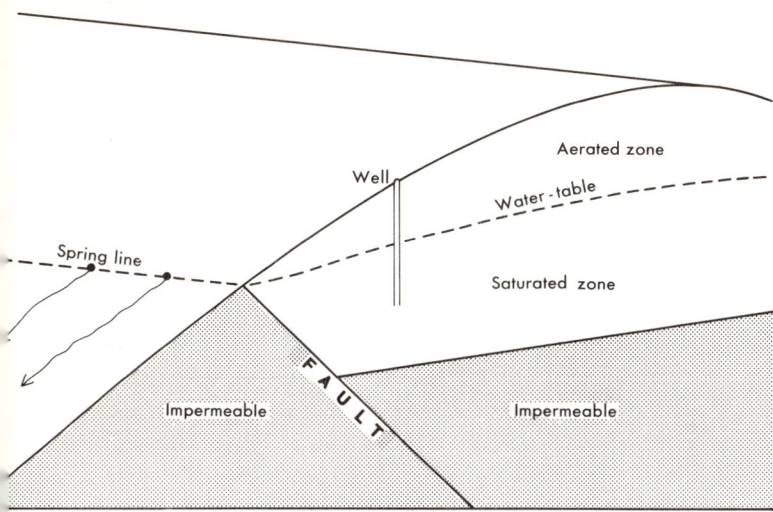

Fig. 86 Water caught by an impermeable rock barrier

will see quite clearly that the level of the water-hole is raised by this to the dotted line as marked, and the line of springs will indicate the line where the fault outcrops on the surface of the hillside. If anyone puts down a well at the place such as is marked, then they will get a good, reliable water-supply that will probably not suffer greatly from drought. The water level in the well will be at the height where the broken line crosses the hole. This is the type of geological structure that is very often looked for when searching for a considerable water-supply, such as for a town.

Fig. 87 shows a spring in Ashwood Dale, just east of Buxton, coming out from such a fault. There is clearly a plentiful supply of water. It is pouring out as a steady

The top surface of the saturated zone is known as the **water-table**. This is not a level surface. It is to some extent sympathetic, as one might say, with the surface of the mountain above.

The zone above it is the aerated or air-filled zone. There may be some water in it, and often after heavy rain the level of the water-table may actually rise and part of the aerated zone may for the time being become part of the saturated zone. Generally speaking, however, the spaces in the aerated zone are not completely filled with water.

There are, of course, many ways in which water may be held underground. It does not always ride on the top surface of an impermeable lower layer. It may be trapped as a great volume of water held in the rock as though it were in a gigantic sponge. This may be due to a fault which may bring impermeable strata up as a block, as is shown in Fig. 86. In this case the fault or crack is water-tight. You

Fig. 87 A spring pouring out at a fault

stream and not merely just as a trickle. In spite of the fact that this is so rapid a flow, it is likely to continue even during fairly dry weather, because of the quantity of reserve contained within the rock.

The public water-supply for towns is sometimes obtained from a river, sometimes from a lake, either natural or artificial, and sometimes from underground. In the case of London about one-fifth of the water comes from chalk lying underneath the city. The chalk hills of the Chilterns in the north, and the North Downs in the south, receive rain which pours on to them and soaks into the chalk itself. This water as it seeps downwards eventually reaches the layer of Gault Clay that lies underneath and is impermeable. The water can sink no farther. As you will see from Fig. 88, the rocks of the Chilterns and the North Downs are one and the same. They are folded downwards in a great gentle curve, called a syncline, beneath the lower Thames basin. Thus the rain falling on these two ranges of hills filters through the chalk to the bottom of this basin, which is known as an artesian basin. If you drill a well-hole anywhere in London through the upper, later, impermeable deposits, you will reach down to the chalk layer and find that you have a supply of water. Again, a structure of this kind is very naturally of the greatest importance to water-engineers.

Clearly, it is possible by various foldings of rock, by various arrangements of faults, and permeable and impermeable layers, to produce an endless variety of types of zones of saturated rock. The few examples we have already described will be sufficient to give the general idea.

Limestone swallow-holes

Limestone regions, although they are, as we have already described, regions of non-porous rock, are particularly permeable because the joints, if they leak at all, soon become widened by the chemical corrosion by the weak acid of the rainwater as it flows slowly through them. The joints, therefore, often become widened sufficiently to justify the term underground cavern. The result of this is that very few rivers flow on the surface in limestone country.

The map shown in Fig. 89 is of Ingleborough in the West Riding of Yorkshire. The top of the mountain, above about 400 metres, is composed of a fairly impermeable rock. As the streams from the summit pass from this on to the surface of the limestone, which forms the flanks of the mountain all around, they one by one sink down into the joints and disappear. They sink until they reach the bottom of the limestone underground, and then they flow on the top surface of the older rock which lies beneath. This is impermeable, and where the junction comes out on to the surface, there most of the streams re-emerge (see the map).

Fig. 90 shows one of these streams entering its swallow-hole. It is Gaping Gill. The cone-shaped entry lying in the fairly level hillside can be seen. It descends vertically for nearly 140 m before it reaches the bottom of a great cavern (Fig. 91).

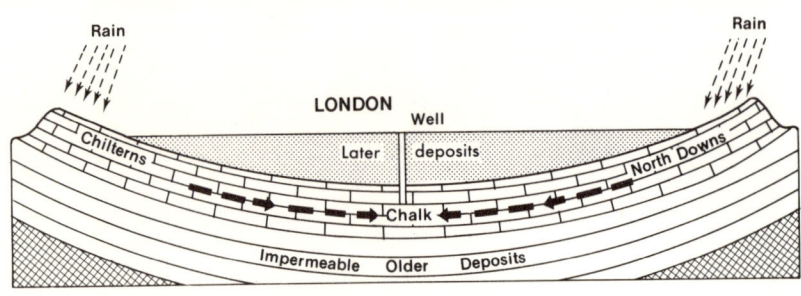

Fig. 88 London water-supply by wells

Fig. 89 Swallow-holes and springs on Ingleborough

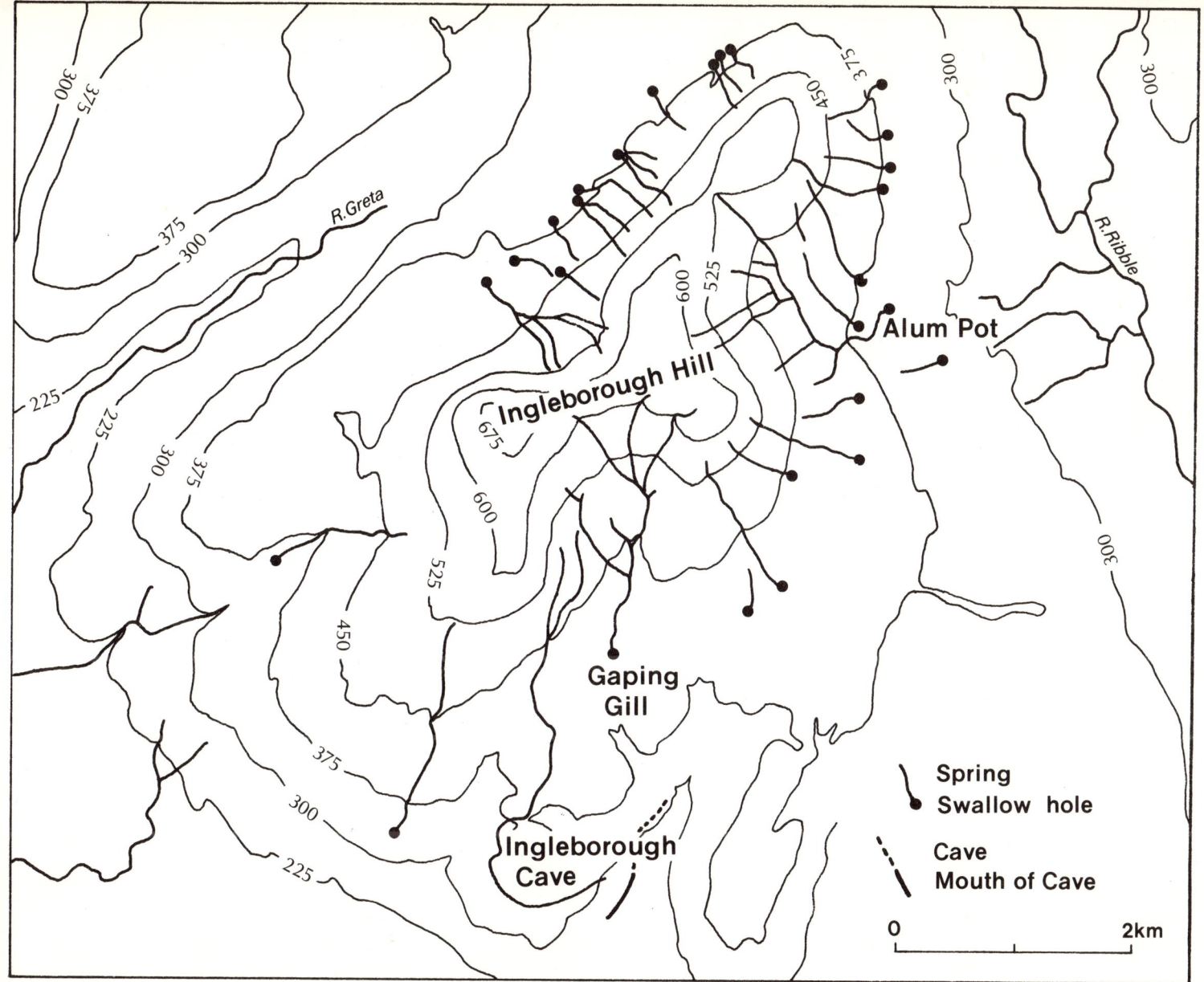

R.Greta

R.Ribble

Alum Pot

Ingleborough Hill

Gaping
Gill

Ingleborough
Cave

Spring
Swallow hole

Cave
Mouth of Cave

0   2km

Fig. 90 A stream goes underground on limestone

Underground caverns

Underground caverns of this type may sometimes be full of water to the roof, but more commonly they now only have a fairly small stream flowing along their floors. They were mostly developed during the times of melting of ice at the end of the glacial periods, when there was much more water about than there is at the present day. Also, as underground streams flow along these quite well-defined courses, they gradually deepen their beds by chemical corrosion and so leave the roof higher and higher above them, as they themselves sink lower and lower.

Very often the roofs of these caverns slowly leak water at the joints. Each drop hovers as it accumulates, and during this pause some evaporation takes place. A little deposit of limestone is left behind. As this continues, a hanging column of deposited rock is built up. This is a stalactite, and a large number of thin, straw-like ones are seen in Fig. 92.

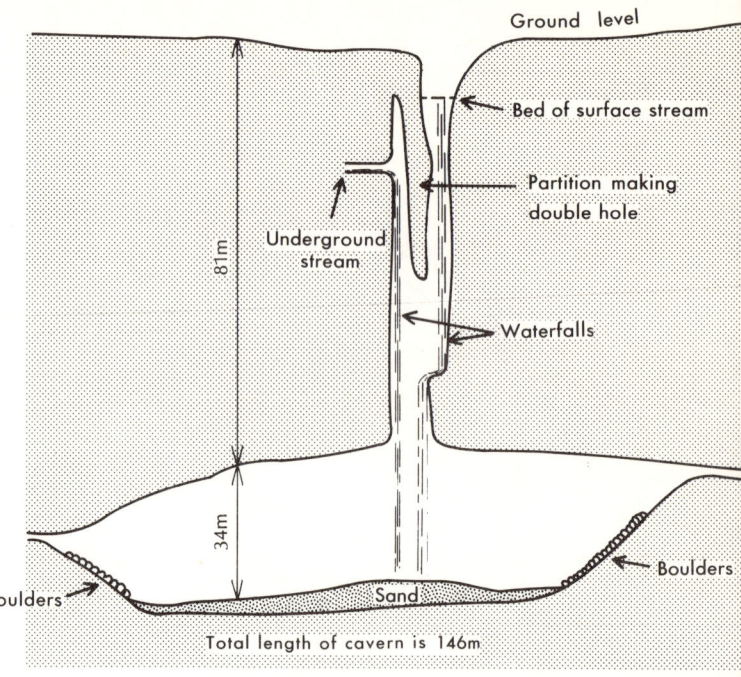

Fig. 91 Gaping Gill hole and cavern

Fig. 92 Stalactites in Mitchelstown Cave, north of Cork

60

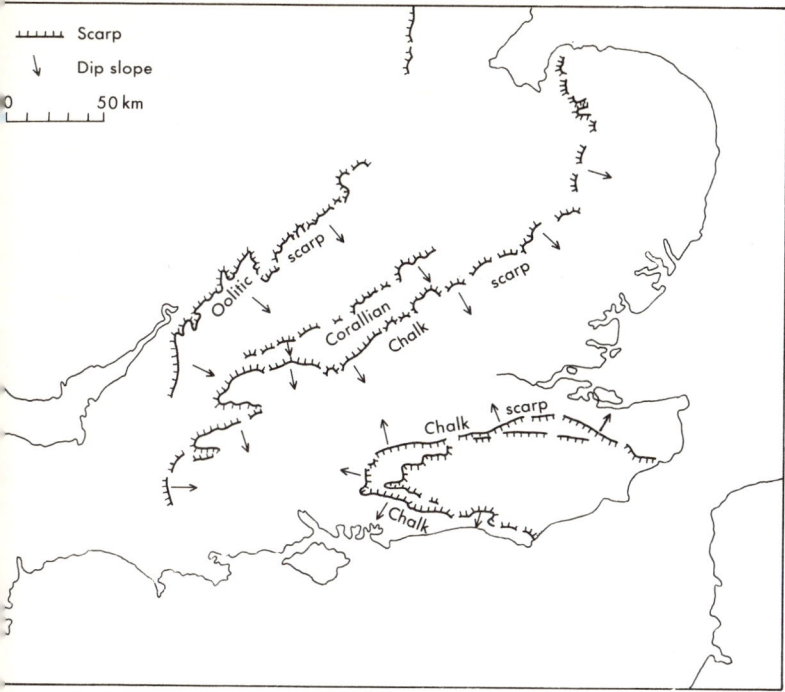

Fig. 93 Escarpments and dip-slopes in southern England

When the drops fall to the ground, they rest for a while. By further evaporation, they may deposit more of their lime. So gradually a column, rather broader than the one from the roof, grows up from the floor. This is a stalagmite.

Dry valleys

In central and southern England, there are several groups of hills consisting either of chalk or limestone, the layers of which slope in one direction, called the dip slope, and which are sharply cut off in the other direction by an escarpment (Fig. 93). Examples of these hills are the North and South Downs, the Chilterns and the Cotswolds. In each case, there are a number of dry valleys on the upper surface of these hills. A photograph of one of them just north of Berkhamsted is shown in Fig. 94 and there is no stream whatever in the bottom of this valley.

An examination of Fig. 95 shows how many have come into existence. As the circumstances are at the moment, the rain falling on the upper part of the hills soaks down into the rocks and finds that it has a base, the impermeable layer of clay, beneath. The level of the water-table in the permeable rock is controlled by the level of the junction of the chalk or limestone and the clay at the point marked A. Water cannot long remain in the permeable rock above this level.

Fig. 94 Dry valley in the Chilterns, Hertfordshire   (*G. R. P. Lawrence*)

The escarpment has come into being by continued erosion, and in times past the position of the escarpment must have been as is shown by the dotted lines. Then the water-table could rise up to the level BCD, and springs would come out at the surface at both B and along the line CD. The one coming out at E produced the river valley we have sketched in.

Now, however, when the escarpment has retreated by erosion to the position A, and the water-table has sunk correspondingly, the spring comes out in the old valley at the position F. The valley is dry from E to F. This is due, in other words, to a lowering of the water-table, owing to a lowering of the outcrop of the junction of the impermeable clay and the permeable rock above.

The North and South Downs and the Chilterns have a very great number of these dry valleys on their surfaces, as any large-scale map will show. There is also a second way in which dry valleys come into existence, and this is as a result of glaciation, when water was forced to flow across ground frozen solid by the icy conditions near glaciers and ice sheets (see Section III, pp. 79–120).

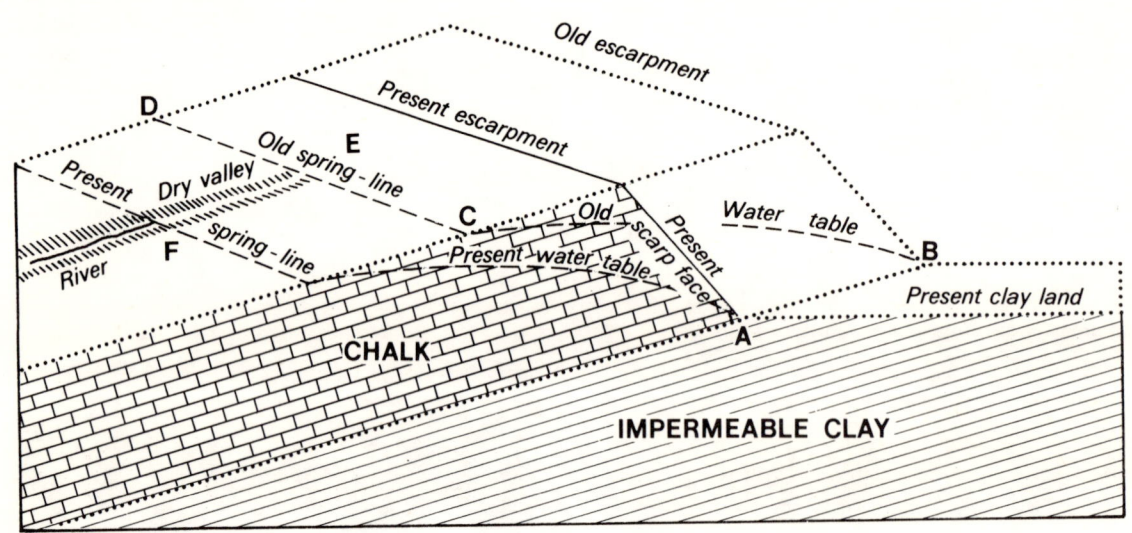

Fig. 95 Dry valleys result from a falling water-table

8   Rivers and their load

Having dealt with the supply of water from the sky, with the ways in which the weather breaks up the solid rock of the mountains, and with the movement of water by underground seepage and channels, we now come to the river itself. In this chapter we shall consider the various ways in which a river is able to erode the ground.

The river can only erode where it touches. That is obvious but often forgotten. There are three possible places: at the head of the river, on the bed of the river, and along its banks. There is nowhere else.

Headward erosion

Erosion at the head naturally means a lengthening of the river. The river will rise farther and farther in the mountains, higher and higher up the hill-side. Fig. 96 shows

Fig. 96 A stream slowly lengthens its course

during the summer the dry source of a small stream on the top of Falcon Crag above Derwentwater. This stream is formed by seepage of water out of the peat that covers this hill-side to a depth of about half a metre. When the water is flowing, the soft material of which the peat is composed will gradually be removed from the semi-circular head of the stream by the moving water. This is a spring. The process is known as **spring-sapping**. The example shown in the photograph is a small one. Spring-sapping can produce very large valley-heads by the continued removal of material that is already loose. The river is lengthening its course.

Vertical erosion

There are four ways in which a river is able to deepen its bed. They are by corrosion, by hydraulic action, by abrasion (sometimes called corrasion), and by attrition.

Deepening by corrosion is doing so by means of chemical action. Naturally this only occurs when the water flows over rocks which can be attacked by whatever chemical there may be present. This is exactly the same as the chemical corrosion of rock that we have already described (pages 52–53). There are other examples on page 60, although there they are underground: here it is exactly the same, except that it is on the surface.

Hydraulic deepening

Hydraulic action is a process which we approached a moment ago in connection with spring-sapping. It involves the removal of material which is already broken up into particles fine enough for the water to be able to transport them. Fig. 97 shows a stream flowing along a path (at the beginning of the climb up Skiddaw from Keswick). A new spring had burst from the side of the hill and flowed down

63

Fig. 97 A mountain-path becomes a stream valley

Fig. 99 Fluted rock bed seen when the stream was nearly dry

Fig. 98 The solid rock bed of an active stream

Fig. 100 Separate smoothed surfaces on the bed of the river Coe

the groove worn by climbers. The material was clay, and, as you see, it had cut quite a deep little model valley for itself and almost all the features of a complete river system. In the foreground, the stream is meandering about on a fairly wide **flood-plain**. All this has been produced entirely by hydraulic action. The whole of the material was already broken up. All the river had to do was loosen it and move it.

In most instances, when we examine a river amongst the mountains we find that hydraulic action has already removed all the finer loose material from the bed of the stream. Fig. 98 shows an example of a stream with a bed of solid rock such as we often see. This particular one is the river Wye above Llangurig in central Wales.

Abrasive deepening

Abrasion is, however, the most important way in which the river can attack its bed. Abrasion is the wearing away of solid rock by rubbing and scraping with sand and pebbles that are being moved by the river. This is a filing, grinding, abrasive action.

The bed of Church Beck near Coniston (Fig. 99) has been grooved by pebbles that were travelling with considerable speed along set paths. A similar pattern can be seen in Fig. 100, which is of part of the bed of the river Coe, dry in summer, in the Pass of Glencoe, Argyllshire. The river normally moves from the top left of the view to the bottom right, and you see three surfaces all smoothed by this abrasion. There is the upper surface with one or two grooves in it, a lower horizontal surface, and an almost vertical one connecting the two. There is a sharp angle between the top surface and the upright one, and this indicates that there must be two separate directions in the water movement. There must be a vertical whirlpool, as shown in Fig. 101, so that water comes across from the left, swirls downwards and backwards, and then rises up. So it abrades the back upright wall with the pebbles and grit that it is carrying.

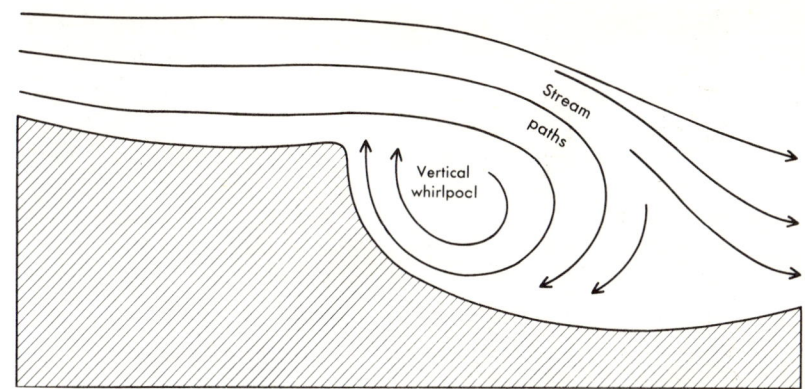

Fig. 101 Intersecting river-currents produce separate surfaces

Potholes

Fig. 102 is a photograph of part of the bed of the river Ure in the North Riding of Yorkshire, when dry during the summer. The spectacle case and the feet give the scale. It is cut into by a number of circular hollows called **potholes**. In two of them in the upper part of the picture you may see through the water that the floor of the hollow is covered with pebbles. This is shown even more clearly in Fig. 103, which is of a rather larger one in the river Wharfe.

These potholes are formed by whirlpools swirling pebbles round in them. They act with a sort of mortar-and-pestle action, which both grinds the pebbles themselves smaller, and makes the pothole wider and deeper. This is an excellent example of abrasion and is perhaps the most successful way in which a river deepens a solid rock bed.

In time, a number of potholes that are near to one another may merge. This is seen at the bottom of Fig. 102, where several fairly shallow potholes have become one larger one. In the common floor of this larger hollow, new potholes have started to form.

Fig. 102 Potholes in the bed of the river Ure

Fig. 103 Pothole about half a metre in diameter in river Wharfe

Attrition

The river, therefore, can either corrode away its bed if the rock is composed of suitable chemicals, can wash it away if it is already broken up, and can cut grooves and hollows in the solid rock by means of the abrasive action of grit and small stones.

Large boulders very often fall into a river from the side. A good illustration of this is in the Aberglaslyn Pass (Fig. 104). Freeze-thaw action very often breaks quite large blocks from the steep sides of the deep valley. They come tumbling down from above and often land in the river, as seen in the photograph. Many of the boulders are more than one metre across. The river cannot move such large masses, but constant bombardment by the pebbles that are being transported by the river breaks off pieces small enough to be moved. So eventually even these large boulders are worn away. This is the process of **attrition**.

When a quarryman wishes to break a large stone that has been blasted from the side of his quarry, he may attack it with his sledge-hammer time after time with no apparent result. Suddenly, however, perhaps after twenty strokes, a huge piece of the rock will fall off. The last stroke was no more powerful than the previous ones, which seemed to have been doing nothing at all. In reality they had been shattering the rock inside, producing microscopic cracks, which eventually were sufficient to allow the piece to break. away. This is exactly what the river does.

Rounding the bend

The river is also in contact with its two banks and material may be removed from them by corrosion, hydraulic action and abrasion.

Fig. 105 shows the river Wye quite near to its source after a dry period. Here the river flows from right to left, making three sharp turns. It erodes the outside of the bank at each corner, and deposits pebbles on the inside. A river is always much deeper on the outside than on the inside of a turn.

When it approaches a curve, a river does not steer. Nor does the water round the corner like a regiment of soldiers making a turn. It takes on a sort of spiral motion, so that it rotates along the length of the stream. The water turns over as well as round.

The resulting downward movement on the outside of the bend increases the speed of the water, and so it can pick up additional material and there is erosion on the outside. The bank is washed away and the bed deepened. Also because of the screw action, the water is moving upwards as it climbs across the shallower part of the stream and the surface on the inside of the bend. So pebbles are deposited there.

Load

Now all these are ways in which the river can erode bed and banks. It still has to move the broken material. It can do so because of its speed. This is controlled by the steepness of

Fig. 104 Tumbled boulders in Afon Glaslyn, Aberglaslyn Pass

Fig. 105 Deposition on the inside of bends, and erosion on the outside

the gradient, and the stiffness of water. We must realise that water has stiffness—**viscosity** the physicists call it.

We are very familiar with the fact that a thick oil, such as is used in a car engine, is a stiff, fairly slow-flowing liquid. In the same way, some liquids have a low viscosity and are very rapid flowing. Petrol is about twice as fluid as water; paraffin about half. Although water is fairly fast, the speed with which it moves down a particular gradient is still controlled by the stiffness.

The faster the water moves, the larger the pebbles that it can roll along the bed, and the more sand, silt and clay can it carry in suspension. Its maximum load is greater. A steep river moves away the broken and eroded material more rapidly than does one whose slope is gentle. The bed is then fairly clear of debris and exposed to the full erosive force of the river. It deepens its bed relatively rapidly.

Rivers move dissolved substances at the full speed of the water. Particles of clay and silt, once tossed into suspension in the water, are so fine that they remain in the midst of the liquid for a very considerable time. They travel to the river mouth nearly as fast as does the water itself.

A river which is flowing rapidly can also move sand in suspension. Most often, however, sand is moved by water rather in the same way as it is moved by wind, by a series of hops. This is technically called a **saltation**—leaping—movement. As each grain of sand lands on the bed of the stream at the end of its hop, it spurts up any grains that it may hit. They in turn perform their leap downstream and when landing toss up fresh grains. So the process goes on, as a sort of relay race. Sand moves to the mouth of the river but very much more slowly than silt.

Pebbles are moved more slowly still. However, substances weigh less in water than they do in air. When you picture the movement of a whole mass of pebbles along a stream-bed, you must remember that beneath the water they weigh only about three-fifths what they do in air.

Small pebbles are rolled along the bed of the stream by the pressure of the water behind them. Larger stones travel by being undermined. The loose material of the bed that may be underneath them is removed and they topple over and so they travel the odd few centimetres down-valley. Eventually also attrition breaks them up into smaller pieces, which can be moved more easily and quickly. All very large boulders await the effect of attrition.

Work has to be done in moving a load downstream. Energy is consumed. The only source of supply for that energy is the speed of the water itself. Consequently, whenever the river picks up additional load, the water loses energy and is slowed down in proportion. There would thus seem to be a maximum load that a river can carry. This will be when all its energy has been absorbed by the task of transport and there is no further energy left with which to pick up more load.

The whole matter is made very complicated, however, by the fact that there is also a minimum velocity necessary to enable a river to move particles of particular size or calibre at all. At a very slow speed a river can move clay and silt, and nothing larger. A little faster and it can pick up sand also. Faster still, it will be moving small pebbles along. And so the calibre that can be carried increases.

When a river which is carrying a mixed load of all sizes slows down, it first drops all the material of calibre too big for the new speed. This has the result that it will probably be able to pick up more load of smaller size. There is an exchange and thus a very strong tendency to move fine material first and leave the larger until later on. If you examine the bed of any stream in the mountains where the water is moving fairly fast, you will find either that it is made of solid rock and all loose material has been moved away already, or if not, then what is lying will be pebbles of fairly large size. All the clay, silt and sand has already gone.

9   Gradient

Fig. 106 shows the river Conway quite near to its source on the moors south of Bettws-y-Coed in North Wales. Here it is not able to deepen its valley very much. This lack of power occurs because there is both very little water and very little solid load in the water. It has very little energy and very few tools. At first it can pick up only the particles of peat, clay and sand that it meets as it flows over the moors. As it goes on, it continues to pick up any loose material that may be about. Now it can start on its processes of abrasion and attrition. Fig. 107 of the same river some kilometres farther downstream shows how it has been able to cut through an outcrop of solid rock. Here it is actively eroding.

Fig. 107 Mountain stream cutting through solid rock

Fig. 106 Small moorland stream in North Wales

Active erosion

As the river goes farther and farther downstream, it becomes even more and more active. It obtains additional water and extra load, and therefore more energy and tools with which to perform more erosion, and more ability to transport the material when it has broken it loose.

Suppose we picture what happens when a river enters a portion that is steeper than the part over which it has just been flowing. Even if the water was already fully laden, when it starts to move down the steeper part it accelerates, and so is able to carry more load (see Fig. 108). It picks up most of the additional load at the place where it first speeds up. There is most erosion at this particular point, Position 1 in the diagram. By the time the river has reached the far end of the steeper reach, the water has taken on so much extra load that once more it is fully laden. No erosion will take place at this lower end.

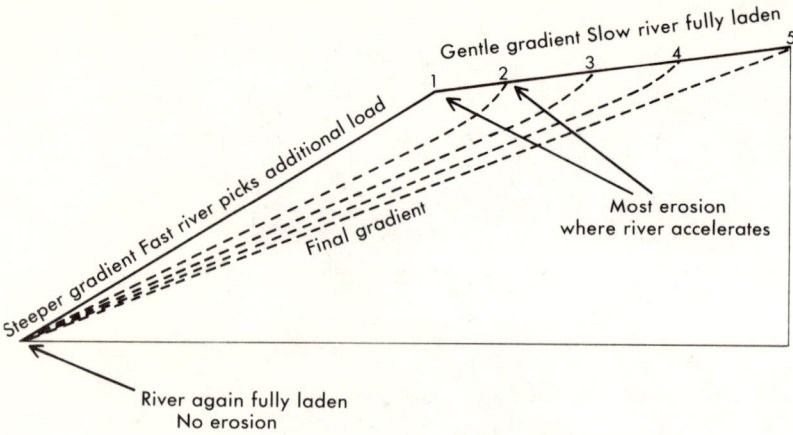

Fig. *108* A river adjusts its slope

Consequently, Profile 1 will in time turn into Profile 2. This still is sufficiently steep to cause erosion, and the same process continues. In time we get Profile number 3, then 4, and then 5. So the irregularity in the slope of the stream has at last been wiped out by this active erosion. This action of making a steep portion of a river bed less steep is known as **de-grading**—decreasing the gradient. It continues until the water is fully laden.

A graded stream

When this has happened the river is in a state of balance and can erode no farther. This does not mean that it carries its load along like passengers in a train. The pebbles that leave one particular stretch are not the same individual ones as just entered it. There is a general forward movement of all the loose material that is in the stream, rather like the movement of people along a queue. There is deposition within the reach, but an equal amount of erosion. Pebbles arrive but others leave. So no net gain or loss occurs. The river is not deepening its bed along this particular portion of its length. The river is said to be **graded**.

Deposition

Now clearly a river which enters the sea, as most do, cannot erode below that level. If it did, the last portion of the river would have to flow uphill! Consequently, the lower portions of the course of a river cannot be deepened to any great extent. The river is working down to what is called a **base-level**, the level of the sea. Below that it cannot go.

If we suppose that the land from the source of the river to the sea started off as a steady slope of the same steepness the whole way, then as erosion cuts into the lower portion, this end of the river becomes less steep than it was at first. It is now less steep than the portion of the river upstream. The water flows slowly along this last stretch of its course and so cannot carry all the load that reaches it. The river is forced to deposit some of the material it is carrying. It takes downstream from the particular stretch less material than enters its upstream end.

Accumulation is taking place. The bed of the stream becomes covered with pebbles, possibly with sand. Sometimes even mud settles out if the water moves sufficiently slowly. The river is then said to be **aggrading**.

The river profile

Summing up, fairly slow erosion takes place near the source of a river. The central portion of the length is the part where most erosion occurs. Here there is a good supply of water, sufficient grit and other abrasive material to make attrition a very active and important process, and yet the river is not so heavily laden as to make it unable to remove the material that it loosens. Finally, near the mouth, deposition probably occurs.

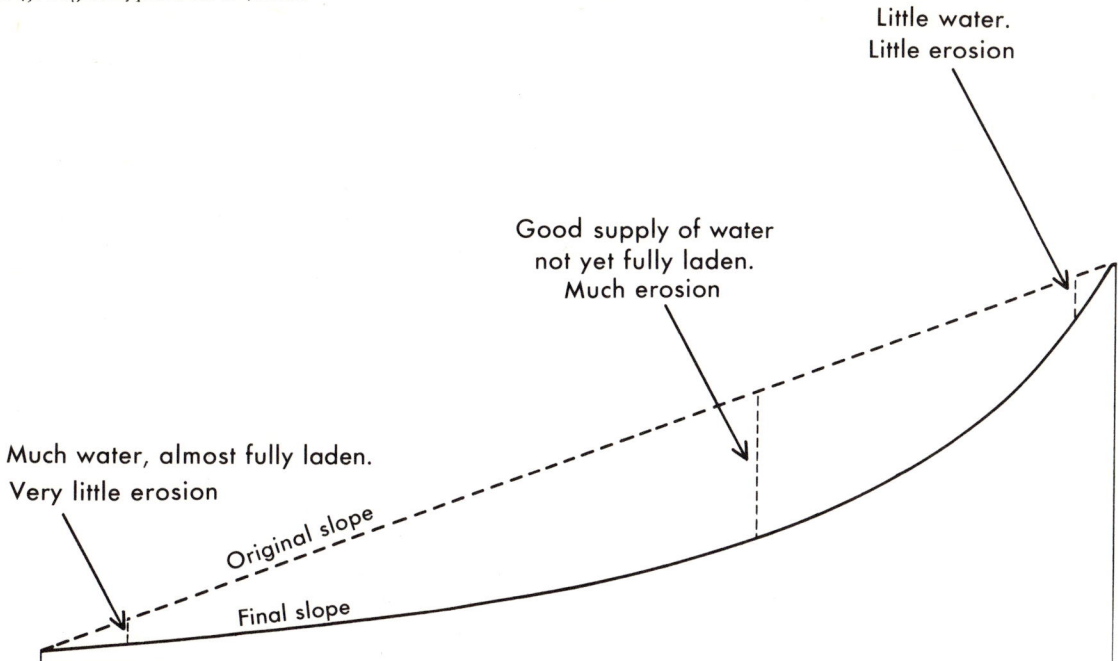

Fig. 109 A typical river profile

Little water.
Little erosion

Good supply of water
not yet fully laden.
Much erosion

Much water, almost fully laden.
Very little erosion

Original slope

Final slope

Thus, if we have a slope with a constant gradient from mountain to sea, most of the erosion occurs in the middle portion and the slope becomes altered to the shape shown in Fig. 109. This is the typical profile of a simple river flowing across rock of the same nature throughout its whole length. Naturally, there are often interruptions in the general flow of the river which may cause irregularities in the course. Examples of such interruptions are waterfalls and lakes.

Strictly speaking, the slope should be different for varying quantities of water, and as the amount changes from day to day according to the weather that has just occurred, so the steepness of all the different parts of the whole length of a river should change from one moment to the next, to match these differing quantities of water. Obviously this is impossible. The river cannot adjust itself as quickly as that. Although we very often say a river is graded, yet it will not necessarily be so on any one day. After a period of dry weather, when there is little water, then a great deal of the load will be dropped. The river is aggrading its bed along almost its whole length. On the other hand, after a period of wet weather, when the river is in spate, or during the melting of snows in the spring and summer if it is that kind of a district, then there is a great deal of water and the river will be flowing rapidly. So it is deepening its bed—degrading it. The actual long-profile of the river is the average of all the various profiles that the river would like to possess on different occasions.

It might be as well to point out that even with the same gradient, the average speed of the water in a river is greater when in spate than in drought. In the latter case, almost all the water is very near the bed or banks, and thus is slowed down by friction with them. Almost all additional water is, however, fairly free from this braking effect, and so flows with much greater speed.

Floods

If a river is fed mainly by surface run-off, the additional water which comes from a sudden rainstorm soon finds its way to the river and a flood will probably occur. If, on the other hand, the river is mainly supplied by underground water from springs, then it will take longer for the extra amount from the rainstorm to filter through. The river will have longer time to cope with the excessive supply of water and so is less likely to flood.

Very often a river is fed by both means and so after a heavy storm it may flood twice. It first of all receives the immediate surface run-off, and then, when that has more or less got away, the water from underground finds its way through and causes a second, later, spate or flood.

There is thus a lapse of time between a rainstorm and when the water actually reaches the river. Floods are particularly severe when this time-lapse is the same over the whole of the catchment area of a river so that all the tributaries become enlarged at the same moment. Then they may all bring large supplies to the main stream together and severe flooding is quite likely to occur. But if the timing for the different tributaries varies, then the main stream will not actually flood, because the excess water-flow is spread over several days.

During floods the river carries a very much greater load than usual. Not only is there more water available, but also a river which is normally quite shallow then flows a great deal faster. This extra speed, as well as the additional water supply, increases the energy in the river, and thus increases its carrying power. Further, the greater depth of water permits the upper layers to brush against parts of the bank that are not normally touched by the river. Loose soil and clay are rapidly washed away. Bushes and trees fall into the river and move down with it. This sometimes makes floods particularly serious.

10   Valleys

We have already found that a river can only erode what it touches. Because of this, the deepening of the bed in the way we have just been describing would produce a narrow gorge, the width of the river itself. This is what does actually happen in districts where the climate is very dry, as in Arizona, where there is the Grand Canyon of the Colorado river. Fig. 110 shows how deep the river has cut.

We are well aware, however, that in Britain most of the rivers lie in V-shaped valleys. Fig. 111 is of a small river to the west of Carlisle.

V-shaped valleys

Fig. 112 shows how this V is produced. The river cuts down a trench equal to its own width. The side wedges, as we might call them, are removed by erosion resulting mainly from the local rainfall. Immediately after a sudden rainstorm, water drains over the whole surface sideways into the river valley. It washes down with it any loose soil that may exist, and starts to knock off the corners of the gorge that might otherwise come into being. Then besides surface sheet wash, rain seeps down through the soil to the river, and drags with it loose material by the process of soil-creep, which was mentioned on page 54. There are also little runnels and small side streams, tributaries of the main river and each doing its share of erosion.

In addition, there is slope collapse. We get steep slopes in various ways. We may have a cliff, a steep-sided U-shaped glaciated valley, a V-shaped river valley, and so on. The rocks that form the steep slopes may be insufficiently strong to hold themselves in position permanently. They lack support on one side. A crack may occur and a landslip

Fig. 110 Deep, narrow Grand Canyon in an arid area (*Aerofilms Ltd.*)

follow, bringing hundreds of tonnes of material down into the valley floor.

In these various ways, the sides are bevelled off and the V-shaped valley produced. The angle of the slope of the V is controlled by the rate at which the rainfall, local drainage and slip can remove the sides compared with the rate at which the river deepens the bed itself. If the river is deepening very rapidly, then the V will be steep. If there is

Fig. 111 V-shaped valley in easily eroded clay

Side 'triangles' the result of local erosion

Central 'rectangle' eroded by the river

Fig. 112 Producing a V-shaped valley

Fig. 113 Afon Rheidol at Devil's Bridge

very little local rain, then the V may become so steep that the valley is practically a gorge. We have already seen this in the Grand Canyon. The Colorado obtains its supply of water from the wet regions farther east, but the canyon itself is in a desert. There is scarcely any local rain, and so although the river continues to deepen its bed, the valley sides are not eroded.

The sides of the V vary from being practically vertical, as in the case of canyons, to being such gentle slopes that the valley may almost be termed a plain. The Ouse valley in the Vale of York, the Dee valley in the Cheshire Plain, and the Thames valley below Staines are good examples. When we are in any of these areas, we scarcely realize that we are in a valley at all.

In a very general way we may say that river valleys have fairly steep sides in the upper middle course and that the sides of the V become gentler as we go downstream. We have already seen the steep V of the valley west of Carlisle (Fig. 111).

The angle is steep in the upper middle reaches, since the river is deepening its bed quite quickly here and local side erosion can only just keep pace with it. The nearer we approach the sea, the slower becomes the deepening. Then the local erosion has more time to erode the wedges, and make the slopes gentle.

Afon Rheidol, east of Aberystwyth, is an excellent example of a very steep-sided valley resulting from very rapid deepening (Fig. 113).

Valleys in limestone

In the British Isles we are not normally troubled by the lack of local precipitation, and so we do not have canyons of the Colorado type in our scenery. We do, however, find steep-sided gorge-like valleys in limestone districts. Burrington Coombe in the Mendips is an example and there are many in the Derbyshire dales.

The rivers in these valleys have deepened their beds in the normal way, but when rain falls on limestone it seeps underground by way of the joints in the limestone, as we have already described on page 52. Consequently, there is very little or no general surface run-off. So the sides of the valley are not eroded away. Many of them are now dry, but they were cut by rivers that flowed when ice was melting at the end of the glacial periods.

It is also possible that a few of these limestone gorges may be the result of cavern-roof collapse, but that is not in general their origin.

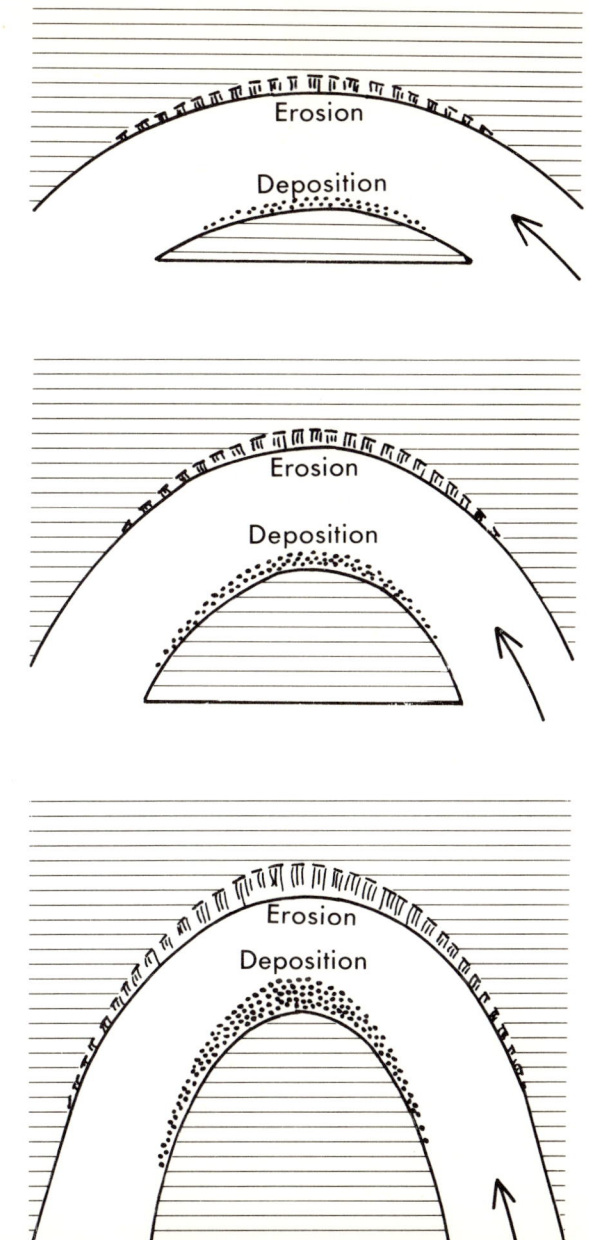

Fig. 114 A bend, once started, becomes sharper

Meanders and flood-plains

In the last chapter we remarked on the fact that the lower part of the course of a river deepened very little, because it is working very nearly down to base level and further vertical erosion is almost impossible.

This means that the river in this portion of its course is moving much more slowly than it is farther upstream. The slow speed makes it easier for the river to wander from a straight course. It drifts from side to side, and soon develops a whole series of meanders.

Fig. 116 A Sussex river meanders slowly to the sea

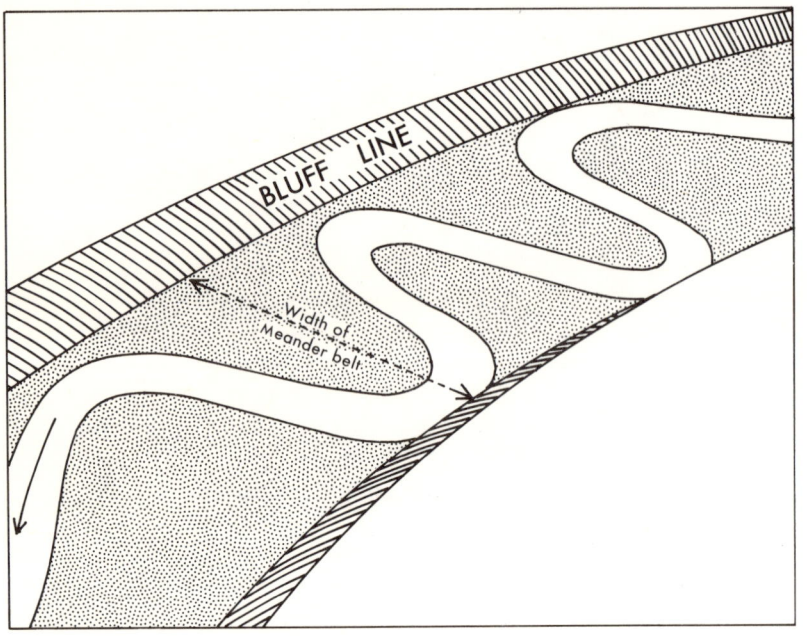

Fig. 115 River-meanders, flood-plain and bluff lines

On page 66 we described how, when a river turns a corner, it erodes on the outside of the bank. If the river starts a turn, then the curve becomes sharper and sharper as time goes on (Fig. 114). A whole series of such corners produces a meandering river (Fig. 115 and Fig. 116 of the river Cuckmere in Sussex).

The width of the swing of these meanders is known as the width of the meander belt (see Fig. 115), and there is a definite maximum for a particular size and speed of river. For the Thames in the London area the width of the meander belt is about four kilometres.

The river erodes as it swings from side to side with the result that the loops of the meanders slowly travel down-valley. The snake, as one might call it, as time has passed, has covered all parts of the width and length of the meander belt on different occasions. This belt is thus lowered to one level. We have the result that is shown in Fig. 115—the

76

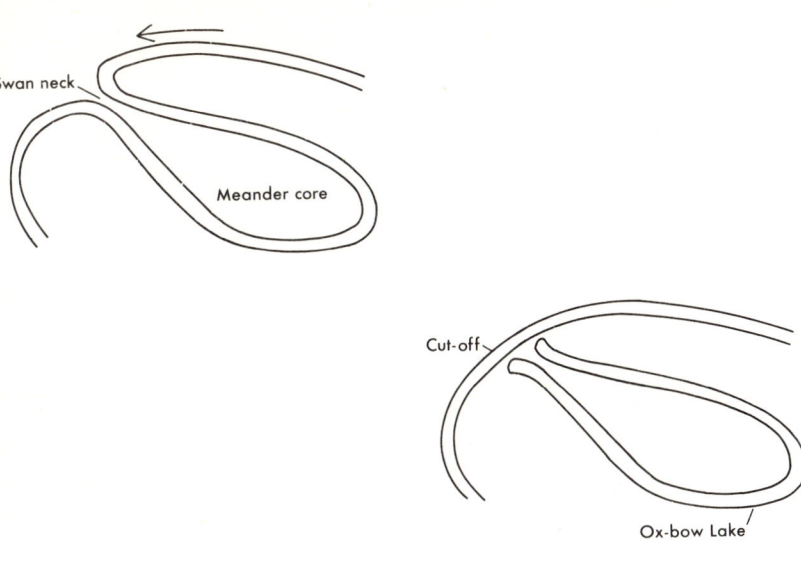

Fig. 117 Meander cut-off and ox-bow lake

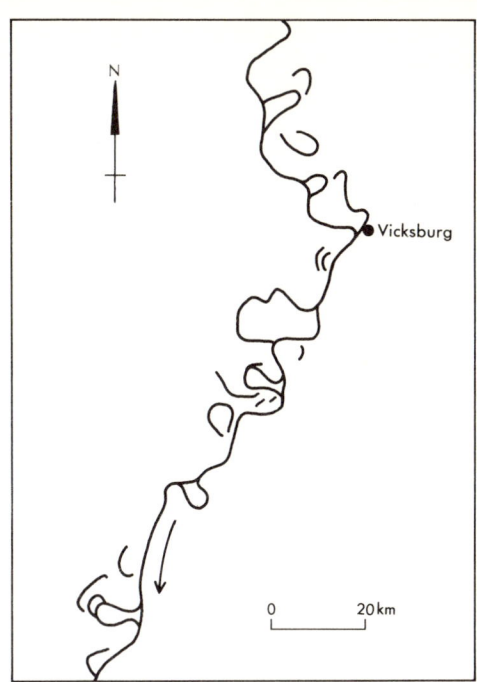

Fig. 118 The lower Mississippi River

level flood-plain with the river lying in it between upright bluff lines. These may be fifty metres or so high, depending on the size of the river, the ease with which the ground is eroded, and its height above the sea.

It is most important to remember that the river has never at one moment occupied the whole width between the bluff lines, excepting perhaps for a few days during a flood. The area between the bluffs has been cut away by changes in the positions of the meanders.

Ox-bow lakes

Sometimes the meanders increase the sharpness of their bends so much (see Fig. 117) that we get a very narrow neck between two particular loops. This is sometimes called a swan's neck. Eventually, when it is in spate, the river erodes right through this narrow neck and the meander is cut off. An ox-bow lake is created in this way.

Most of the flow of the water now goes by the direct route, which is shorter and therefore steeper, and very little flow passes round the old meander loop. The water becomes more or less stagnant there, and ridges of sand and shingle begin to build up across the entrance and exit of this U-shape. In time it becomes a *morte* or dead lake. Gradually with the aid of reeds and other vegetation, and by slumping of the banks, it fills up and disappears. Fig. 118 shows numerous examples of ox-bow lakes on the Mississippi river.

English rivers

We should remember that the rivers in England are not only very much smaller than those in most parts of the world, because of the small size of the country, but that they are also almost all in a very unnatural state. The country is so densely populated and so intensively used that the rivers are controlled to a great extent. Narrow meander necks are artifically cut off. Weirs are built to control the level of the water so as to keep an agreeable and useful river. The Thames is controlled by weirs for the whole of its length between Lechlade and Teddington. One of the weirs is at Pangbourne, near Reading, and is shown in Fig. 119.

Fig. 119 Water-flow control in the Thames at Pangbourne

Section Three:

The Work of Ice

11   The characteristics of ice

Snow, ice, glaciers, ice sheets, icebergs, the cold parts of the Earth's surface, are not necessarily so very cold as we may at first imagine. At the height of the Ice Ages, it was no more than about six degrees Centigrade cooler than it is today. The Ice Ages might truly be said to be still present in places like the Alps and Scandinavia—which are both very popular holiday areas. At the moment the area of ice in the world is about a third of what it was at the maximum of the most widespread glaciation.

The causes of ice ages

Temperature determines whether or not a place will be covered by ice. It is necessary, of course, for snow to fall on the area, but the temperature controls the rate of thaw and this is more important than the rate of fall.

Numerical measurements show that the average winter temperature of most of Europe and North America has risen by about one degree Centigrade during the last seventy years. The rise has not been a steady one—there have been several warm and several cool spells within the seventy years. Direct surveys have proved quite clearly that glaciers shrink during the warmer times, although the amount of snowfall does not alter very greatly. Swiss glaciers now cover only about three-quarters the area they did seventy years ago.

We naturally wonder what it is that causes these changes in temperature. We should first examine what we definitely know. We have already noted that temperatures have risen during the last seventy years, although with occasional set-backs, but on the other hand plant fossils seem to suggest that there has been a general lowering of temperature during the last seventy million years in Europe at least.

During the last fifteen or so million years, earth-movements have raised mountain ranges by a thousand or more metres above their previous level, and the average height of the land surface is more than doubled. The ocean depths must naturally have sunk a corresponding amount, for the volume of the Earth has not changed. The irregularities on its surface have merely become bigger.

There are two ways of reaching a cold climate—either by going towards the Poles, or by climbing a high mountain. There is snow today at the Equator at 430 m. Because the Earth was cooling, the snowline was coming down, and the land areas, especially the younger mountains like the Alps, the Himalayas, the Rockies and the Andes, were climbing up towards it. After they had met, the Ice Ages started.

Both these changes continued without much reversal, and so they could only produce a single ice age; what has actually occurred during the last half million years is, in fact, a succession of four or five ice ages, with periods in between that were generally as warm as, or even warmer than, the present. Something more, then, is required to explain these irregular, alternating effects.

The whole Earth cools and warms. This must mean a variation in the quantity of heat reaching the surface. Probably the amount radiated by the sun changes, but exact measurements have not yet been made over a sufficiently long number of years to enable us to be very definite about this. The quantity of heat received does, indeed, vary from one year to the next by a small amount. There is a certain rhythm in this, apparently connected with sunspots, but this only shows that a long-period variation is a possibility, and it goes no way at all towards telling us that it has actually taken place.

At the moment, therefore, we have far too little knowledge to be very certain about the causes of the individual Ice Ages.

From snow to ice

Snow is ice in a very lacy, feathery form. As it lies on the ground in this condition it is three or four times as bulky as the water it would make if melted. Slowly the finest plumes of the crystal-points evaporate. Some of the vapour condenses again on the cores of the crystals, making them rather more solid. In this form it is known as powder snow.

This process continues, perhaps with a little actual thawing and re-freezing. The texture of the snow gradually changes into something like a sponge. The separate crystals have mostly merged together, but there are still a great many air-channels, and these all communicate with one another in just the same way as do the channels in an ordinary sponge. When it has reached this stage, it is known as **firn** or **névé**, and because there is rather less air than at first, it is now just about half the weight of the same volume of water. This is the sort of condition you will find if snow has lain on the ground for some time. You will realize that it is no longer anything like the soft, fluffy material that fell during the snowstorm.

The changes do not stop. The firn becomes more compact, perhaps aided by a certain amount of pressure from additional snow that may be now lying on the earlier fall. Liquid water, from slight thawing of the upper surfaces during the day-time, slowly flows through the air-channels in the firn. Some of this water freezes in these channels and chokes them up, so that we soon reach the stage when the material is no longer porous. It still contains a certain amount of air, but this is in the form of individual bubbles, separated from one another by ice instead of in the form of through-channels. At this stage it is first called 'ice', and because of the mixture of air with it, it is white in colour. It is about four-fifths as heavy as water.

If the white ice happens to form part of a glacier or an ice-sheet, the pressures on it either whilst it is forced along, or because of the weight of other snow and ice on top, gradually squeeze the remaining air out of it. It becomes fully formed **glacier ice**, and is just about eleven-twelfths the weight of water. The whiteness has gone, and it has the true colour of pure, solid ice. It is a gloriously clear, clean-looking, pale sky-blue, ice-blue, and to see this in bright mountain sunlight is to see one of the most beautiful colours in the world.

Melting temperature

The temperature at which ice melts is zero degrees Centigrade. That is when it is under atmospheric pressure. If the pressure increases, it melts at a lower temperature. The pressure due to the weight of 200 m of ice is sufficient to lower the melting-point by $\frac{1}{8}°$ C., and so if the ice in a glacier at this depth is to remain solid its temperature must be this much below zero.

It is only possible to slide and skate on ice because of this effect, which is called **regelation**. The additional pressure of your weight is sufficient to melt the ice beneath you, without raising its temperature. There is a thin film of water between your foot or skate and the ice, and this acts as a lubricant and enables you to slide or glide along. The water freezes again just as soon as you remove the pressure.

Anyone who walks on snow on a rough path partially melts it at each stride. The water falls into the crevices of the path, it freezes again as he continues his walk, and so a footprint of ice is left securely anchored to the path by little teeth of ice extending into every little hole in its surface. That is why it is so difficult to sweep the snow away after people have walked on it.

Moving ice

Exactly the same kind of thing happens in a glacier when the ice tries to move downhill. All kinds of pressures are set up when it approaches a bend in the valley or a narrow part. These pressures cause temporary thawing of thin films within the glacier, so that the ice on the two sides of the thaw can slide on itself and behave for the time being as though it were no longer one piece. When the pressure is removed, the ice freezes together again.

It is also known that ice which is 60 m or more down below the surface is not the hard, brittle substance to which we are accustomed. The total pressure is now more than six atmospheres and the ice becomes a semi-plastic or slightly flexible substance, somewhere between a liquid and a rigid solid. It is fairly easy for it to 'flow' under these conditions. Laboratory experiments have proved this, and the ice at the end of a glacier generally shows that it has been bent in all sorts of ways that would be quite impossible whilst it was brittle.

The movement of a glacier is produced by the fact that the valley slopes downhill, but unlike a river, its stiffness enables it to move uphill for short distances by being pushed from behind, in the same way as a train may have the engine at the rear. Glaciers can therefore ride over rock barriers up to one hundred metres in height, as we shall see later.

Ice sheets gradually move outwards in very much the same way as a pool of thick cream gradually spreads in an ever-widening circle on a perfectly level table. The weight of the accumulation at the centre drives the edges outwards.

The rate of movement is very variable indeed. The centre of a glacier moves faster than the sides or bottom, because the latter are slowed down by rubbing on the rock sides and floor of the valley. Some glaciers move centimetres a year, a few at 30 m a week, but a good average figure to think of is probably about 30 cm a day. Ice sheets move very much more slowly, and perhaps it might be correct to say that the faster parts only move a metre or so a year, whilst the centre of the sheet scarcely moves outwards at all.

12   The head of a glacier

When a patch of snow on the mountain-side lasts throughout the year and never melts completely away, it greatly encourages the weathering process known as **freeze-thaw**. The snow becomes firn, and when some of it thaws during a warm day the melt-water finds its way into all the crevices in the rocks on which it lies. As it freezes at night, it expands and so gradually wedges out pieces of rock and breaks them up. This especially happens near the edges of patches of firn, and so the shallow hollow, which had first caused the snow to collect, gradually becomes deeper and its sides are steepened. This process is known as **nivation** (see Fig. 120).

Fig. 120 A hollow on the mountain-side deepens by freeze-thaw

If the area of firn becomes deeper, some of it turns to ice and a tiny ice sheet comes into existence. It may continue to grow. The weight of the ice then becomes sufficient for a sliding movement to occur. A small glacier has been formed and the broken material is transported away whilst the freeze-thaw action continues on the back and side walls. It very often happens that thaw and freeze causes the ice to become anchored firmly to the walls of rock, and so when the ice moves away a powerful plucking action occurs. By now the hollow has become much deeper and the ice on the

Fig. 121 Cwm Idwal in Snowdonia

main part of the floor is sliding across the surface of the rock. A dragging, grinding action occurs at this part.

The semi-circular hollow that has been created in the mountain-side in this way is called a **cirque** in France, **cwm** in Wales, or **corrie** in Scotland. There is no English word for the feature and all three names are used equally often. Fig. 120 shows five stages in the formation of a cirque in this way.

Cirques

The back wall is always very steep and often high. The back of Cwm Idwal (Fig. 121) is a precipice of nearly 600 m, which is more than half the total height of the mountain. The loose scree has come into existence in post-glacial times by freeze-thaw action on the exposed rock walls of the cirque.

Naturally a cirque forms at the upper end of a river valley that existed in pre-glacial times. The ice which moves away from such a cirque becomes the main valley glacier. It gains additional snow from avalanches from all sides, and additional ice from tributaries. It is then a large, fully-formed glacier. Glaciers tend to become very large quite near to their sources, and because the erosive power of ice largely depends upon its weight, the long-profile of the old river valley becomes altered to the new shape shown in Fig. 122. Whilst the source is greatly deepened, the part

occur along it, but these will be discussed in the next chapter. The up-valley end is a true cirque, although it is often referred to as a 'valley-head'. Fig. 123 shows Mickleden, the head of Great Langdale valley. The glaciers started from these steep walls and moved away from them down the valley.

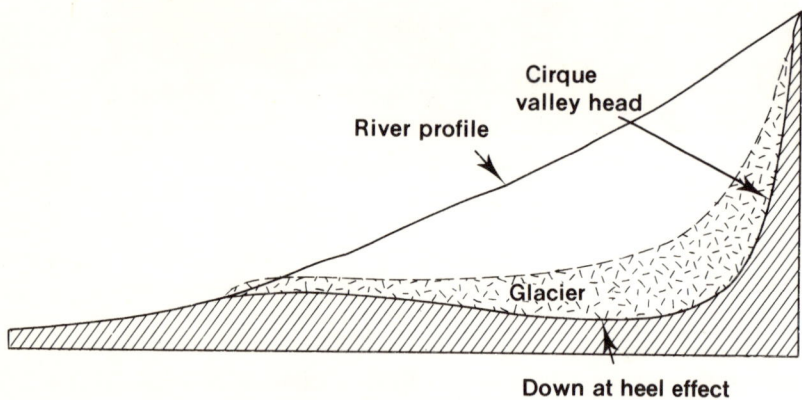

Fig. 122 A river profile is altered by a glacier

Fig. 123 The head of the Great Langdale valley, Cumbria

of the valley where the ice is thickest is eroded most. At the same time the lower part of the valley, where the ice is gradually becoming less in quantity because of melting, is eroded much less, and, naturally, glacial erosion stops completely at the snout.

The total result of this is that the rock floor under the glacier tends to be inclined uphill as we go down-valley from the point of maximum ice. This produces a kind of 'down-at-heel' effect. The profile shown in Fig. 122 refers to the whole length of the glacier. Various irregularities

Perched cirques

When the firn patch forms in a hollow in the side, instead of at the end, of a main valley, it leads to a cirque which contains only a very short glacier, tributary to the main one. The quantity of ice in this is very much less than in the valley itself, and so the floor of the latter is deepened by the grinding action of the glacial erosion much farther than is the floor of the tributary.

When eventually the ice all melts away, we are left with a semi-circular hollow in the valley-side with its floor some way up above the main floor level (see Fig. 124). A cirque of this kind is formed in exactly the same way as the main, valley-head type of cirque. The only difference is that its glacier was smaller than the main one, and so did not erode so deeply. It should be termed a 'perched' or 'hanging' cirque. It has the appearance of a giant's arm-chair, with high back and arms. The giant sits in the floor of the cirque, and his feet are in the bottom of the main valley.

So long as the main glacier is present in its valley, the small tributary falls down on to it, but at the last stages, when much of the ice has melted away, the tributary becomes so short that its ice terminates at the lip of the perched cirque. This stage is shown in Fig. 125. The rock, which the short glacier plucks from the back wall and erodes from the floor, is now dropped from the melting ice at the mouth of the cirque, and forms a terminal moraine (page 104).

In addition, the thinning of the ice results in less erosion of the floor near the mouth. The same down-at-heel effect as occurs with a main glacier now occurs also with the tributary.

When we examine a perched cirque from which the ice has completely melted away, we almost always find this rock hollow, which is made deeper still by the presence of the moraine across the mouth. Consequently, most cirques now have their floors partly occupied by 'cirque lakes'. Fig. 126 of a cirque north-west of Ffestiniog in Merionethshire is an example. The steep back and side walls, the rock barrier across the mouth of the cwm, and the lake occupying the hollow, all show clearly.

Arêtes

Naturally a mountain-side gives rise to a number of these cirques when it is being glaciated. This occurred on Snowdon (Fig. 127). The glaciers forming in the two

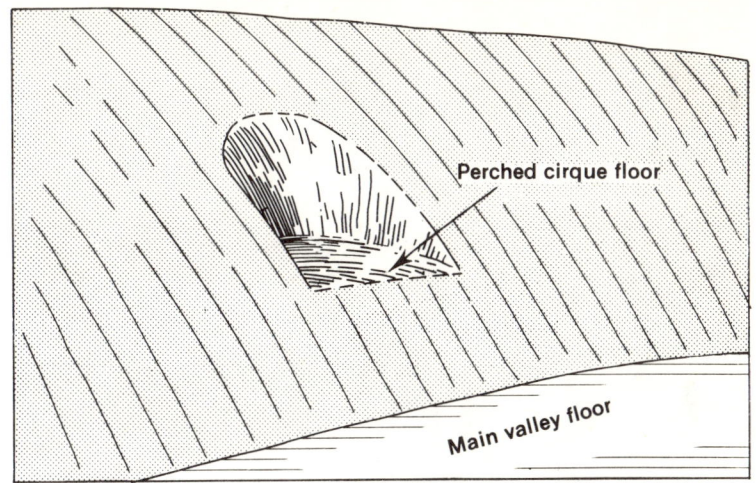

Fig. 124 A cirque perched on the valley-side

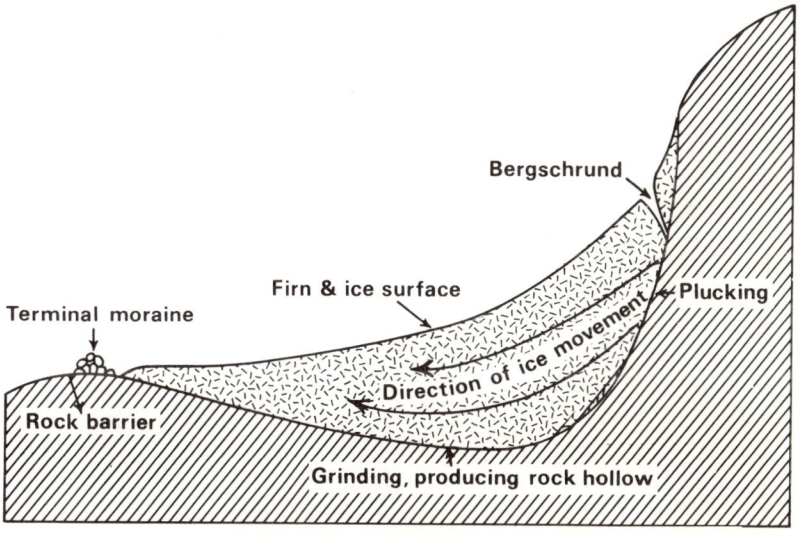

Fig. 125 A cirque glacier

85

Fig. 126 A lake fills the hollow in a cirque

Fig. 128 Striding Edge, an arête between two cirques (*Aerofilms Ltd.*)

Fig. 127 Twin cirques on Snowdon (*Aerofilms Ltd.*)

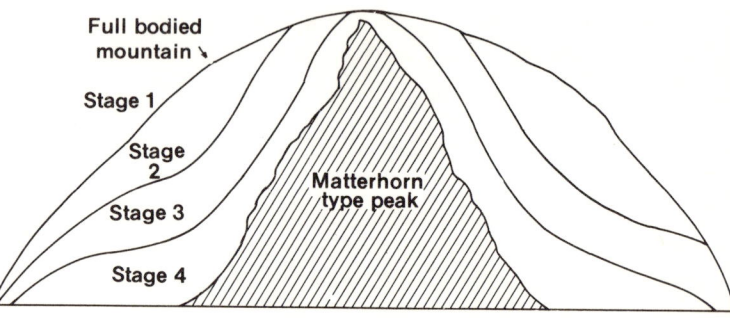

Fig. 129 Cirques eat away at a mountain mass

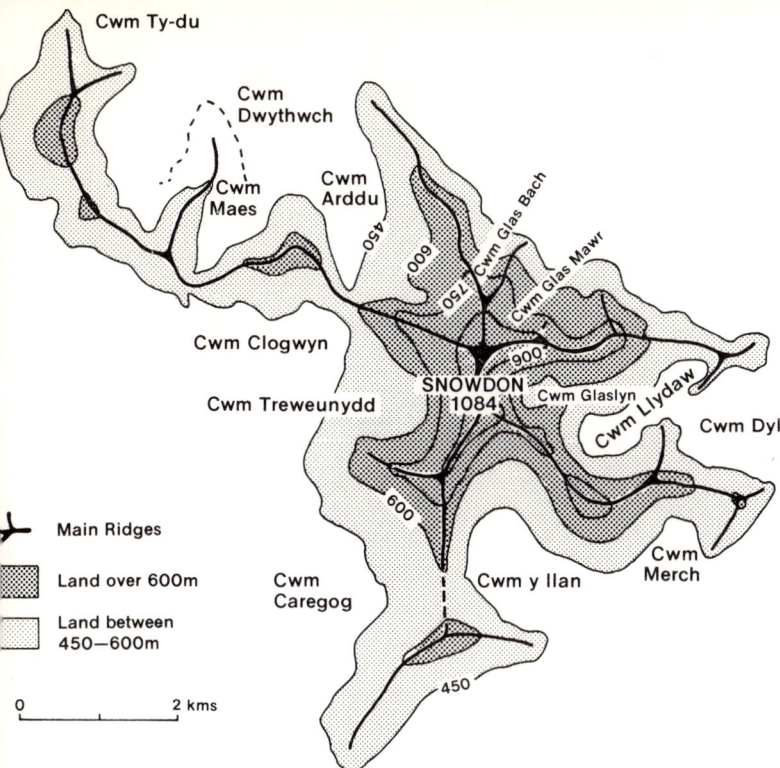

Cwm Ty-du

Cwm
Dwythwch

Cwm
Maes

Cwm
Arddu

Cwm Glas Bach

Cwm Glas Mawr

450

600

750

900

Cwm Clogwyn

SNOWDON
1084

Cwm Glaslyn

Cwm Llydaw

Cwm Dyli

Cwm Treweunydd

600

450

Cwm
Caregog

Cwm y llan

Cwm
Merch

✈ Main Ridges

▨ Land over 600m

▦ Land between
450–600m

0   2 kms

Fig. 130 The rides and cwms (= cirques) of Snowdon

something whose map has a very spidery look. Fig. 130 shows the ridges which are all that remain of the one-time 'solid' mountain. Before the glaciation, the deep cwms did not exist. There would be only short, very much smaller, V-shaped river valleys starting at springs in the mountain-side. Glaciers began in all these hollows and enlarged them to the size they are now.

The presence of all these various cwms with the ridges between them makes the district very attractive, not only from the scenic point of view, but also because of the large number of rock climbs that can be found up the arêtes and the back walls.

When cirques occur on opposite sides of a mountain, their back walls often approach so near to one another that the whole mountain is reduced to a mere ridge. The crest-line becomes very irregular and, in the extreme case, all that is left is a great pointed peak or **horn**, such as is the case with the Matterhorn (4505 metres), seen in Fig. 131. This particular mountain is so striking in this manner, that whenever a similar horn-shaped peak is described, it is referred to as a Matterhorn-type of summit.

Fig. 131 The Matterhorn on the Swiss-Italian frontier
(*Swiss National Tourist Office*)

cirques are so near to one another that only a narrow ridge of rock is left between. This is known as an **arête**. Striding Edge, on the eastern side of Helvellyn (Fig. 128), shows the appearance after the ice has melted away. On the left is Red Tarn, still with its cirque lake, and Nethermost Cove is on the right beyond the arête. Both these are cirques.

A mountain which in pre-glacial times was a great rounded, full-bodied mass can become reduced to a mere fragment of its original bulk by the production of a large number of cirques. Fig. 129 shows this change in four stages. The great pile of Snowdon has been reduced to

87

13   The course of a glacier

The best known effect on the scenery resulting from glaciation is the U-shaped valley. This is the most obvious and dramatic result. Of course, the U-shape only becomes a valley after the ice has melted away, for during the ice period it forms the bed and banks of the glacier. It is, then, U-shaped in much the same way as are the bed and banks of a straight river.

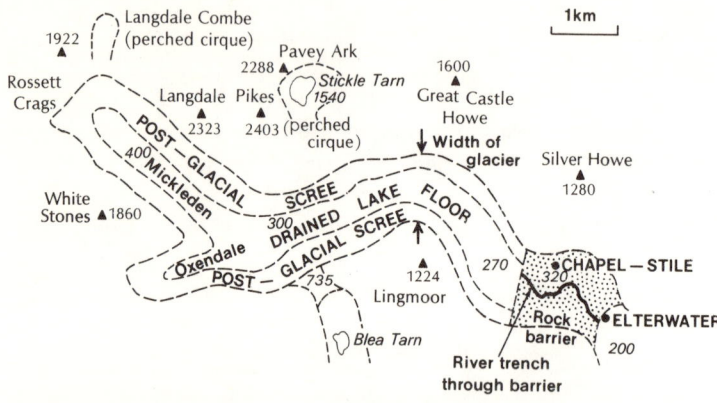

Fig. 132 The Great Langdale valley, Cumbria

U-shaped valleys

The Great Langdale valley in the Lake District is a well-known valley of this kind (see Fig. 133). Very little of the solid rock side is seen in this photograph, but it does outcrop just below the 500-metre contour as is shown in the key, Fig. 134. These crags, and others farther up-valley, are a favourite ground for rock climbers. The lower parts of the sides of the U are covered over by falls of broken rock which have built up great slopes of screes on both sides.

Fig. 133 Langdale Pikes and the Great Langdale valley

There was a river valley here before the glaciation. Portions of the sides of the V of this valley still remain as the rather gentler slopes of the upper part of the mountain about 500 m. They have been only slightly altered by freeze-thaw and other weathering during and since the Ice Ages (Fig. 135).

The glacier adopted the valley that already existed, deepened it by its dragging and bulldozing action and so formed the U shape, as seen in Fig. 135 B. Whilst the glacier was present, the U portion was filled with ice up to the level indicated, and so the nearly vertical rock side-walls were supported by the fact that it was rock-ice-rock across the valley.

When, however, the ice at last melted away, it was rock-air-rock (see Fig. 135 C), and the steep sides of the U, no longer supported, partly collapsed and nearly choked the valley with scree. Most of this scree fell quite soon after the passing of the ice, but present-day freeze-thaw action

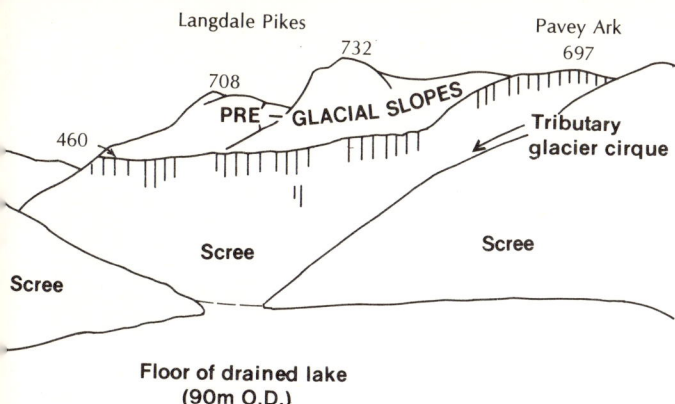

Floor of drained lake
(90m O.D.)

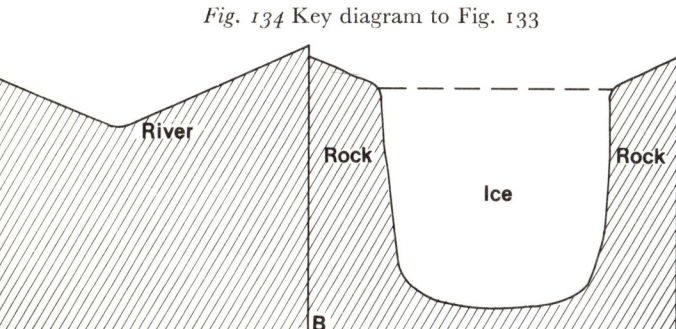

|||| Exposed rock
||||| slides of U valley

Fig. 134 Key diagram to Fig. 133

Fig. 135 The change from a V- to a U-shaped valley

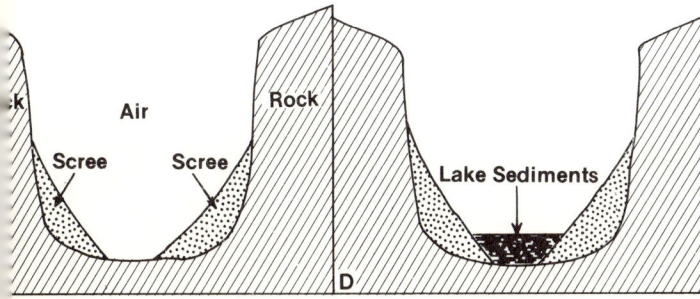

A U-shaped valley when the glacier melts away

does occasionally add a little more to it. The screes are quite striking features of the Langdale valley. They are mostly covered with pasture and are sufficiently stationary to make it safe to build the road and most of the farm-steads on them.

There is a fourth surface in this valley, the flat floor (Fig. 135 D). Immediately after the melting of the ice, this portion of the valley became flooded with water and formed a lake. Pebbles, sand and mud fell to the bottom of this lake and created the level area of the centre of Fig. 133, which became visible after the lake had drained itself away.

The size of a glacier

In the case of the Langdale valley, the U is at least 350 m deep (Fig. 134) and about 750 m wide from solid rock to solid rock. This gives a cross-sectional area more than a quarter of a million square metres for the glacier. If we suppose that it had an average velocity of three metres a week, which is a possible kind of figure for a glacier in such a position, we have the result that nearly one million cubic metres of ice would pass any particular point each week.

We have no knowledge of the amount of snow falling in glacial times and whether or not it was equivalent to the rain that falls today, but it is by no means unreasonable to suggest the large size for the glacier.

If we had any remaining doubts we have only to look at glaciers that exist today, such as the Suphelle (pronounced *soo-pella*), north of the Sognefjord (Fig. 136). This is very similar to the size that the Langdale glacier must have been, and it fills in the whole of its U shape, so that only the more gently sloping tops of the mountains show above the ice. In this photograph the fraction of mountain that is visible rises about 250 metres above the glacier and no one knows how deep is the ice.

Fig. 136 A deeply crevassed glacier filling its U-shaped bed

Spur erosion

Although a glacier is surprisingly flexible, and can turn
fairly sharp corners (see Figs. 132 and 137), it still tends to
remove any obstruction that projects from the side of the
valley. So gradually it straightens its path. Any spurs which
interfere with the direct flow of the glacier tend to be cut
away, so that they become what is called 'truncated'.
There are a number of these in Kentmere, west of Kendal,
as are seen in Figs. 138 and 139. Beyond the rock barrier, in
the cirque, is Kentmere reservoir, an artificial restoration
of the one-time natural cirque lake.

The long-profile

The long-profile of a glacier differs completely from that of
a river, as we have already seen (page 84). As it moves
along its upper reaches, a glacier grows larger and larger,
both by additional snow falling directly upon it, by fresh
avalanches down its sides, and by union with tributary
glaciers.

Fig. 137 The Fiescher glacier in the Berner Alps, Switzerland
(Swiss National Tourist Office)

90

Fig. 138 Truncated spurs in the glaciated Kentmere valley

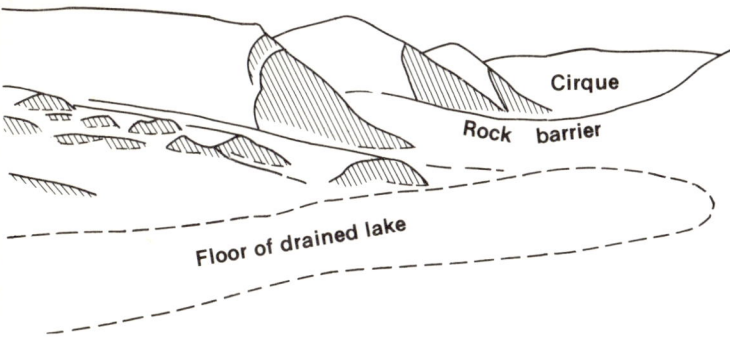

Fig. 139 Key diagram to Fig. 138

All the time, it is descending to lower levels, and probably to a warmer climate. Melting starts. There comes a point along the length of the glacier beyond which loss by thaw is greater than the gain of ice. From this point onwards the glacier gradually becomes smaller.

If, as we will suppose for the moment, the valley is the same width all the way, then the glacier thickens from its source to the balance point, and then slowly becomes thinner. This produces the down-at-heel profile that we discussed in the last chapter.

Rock barriers

This profile belongs to an ideal glacier whose valley is supposed to be the same width all the way. This does not occur in reality, and whenever the valley narrows there is usually both a thickening and an increase in the speed of movement as the ice is forced through. To move the same quantity of ice past two particular points the three measurements, width, depth and speed, must multiply together to make the same answer in both cases, so that if one, the width, becomes smaller, either or both of the other two must become larger.

Thus there are changes in both depth and speed from point to point. The former alters the erosive power and so the slope of the rock bed alters. 'Rock barriers' result where there is little erosion. They are great, natural dams, stretching right across a glaciated valley. We have already seen one in Fig. 138. A well-known one blocks the valley between Grasmere and Rydal Water (Fig. 140), one crosses the north end of Nant Ffrancon, another crosses the Langdale valley at Chapel Stile (Fig. 132). Rock barriers are very common features of all glaciated valleys.

Naturally they cannot be seen when the glacier itself is actually in the valley. They often rise between thirty metres and one hundred metres or even more above the level of the rock floor up- and down-valley of them. They are much more controlled by the erosive power of the glacier than by the strength of the rock, and do not particularly occur where the rock is more resistant to erosion.

The rock barrier at the northern end of Loch Ness keeps the sea out and makes the loch a freshwater feature instead of a fjord. The barrier is approximately 250 m above the level of the floor of the loch (barrier 30 m, above sea-level; loch floor, 215 m below). The fact that a glacier passed over this shows clearly that ice can be pushed up-hill to a remarkable extent.

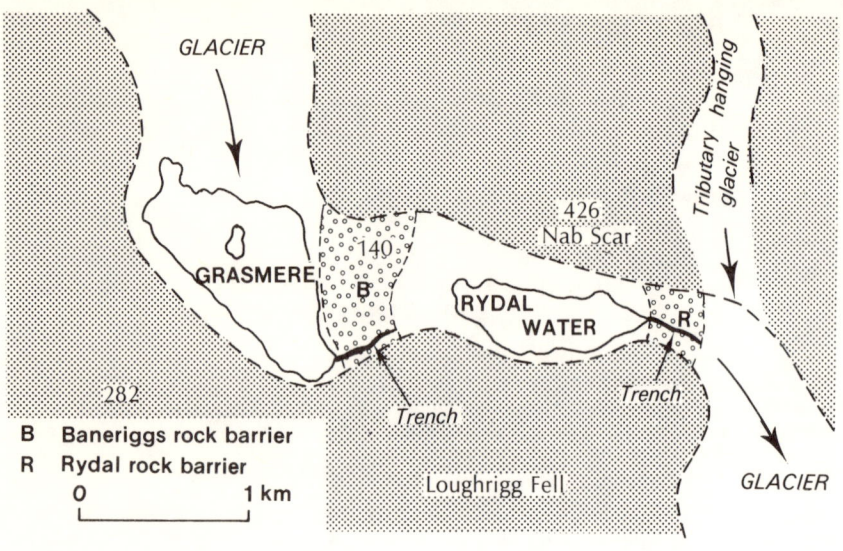

Fig. 140 The rock barrier between Grasmere and Rydal Water

B   Baneriggs rock barrier
R   Rydal rock barrier

0   1 km

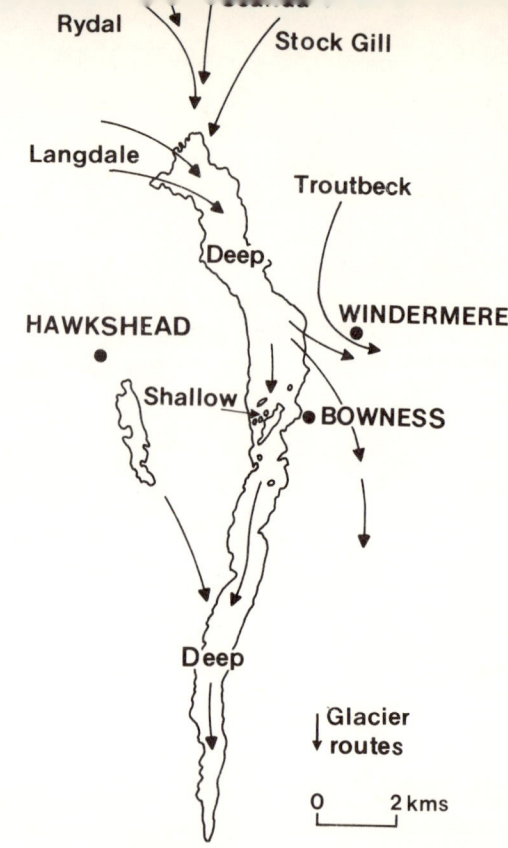

Fig. 141 The glaciers in the Windermere area

Glacier routes

0   2 kms

As these barriers are complete dams, they lead to the formation of lakes on their up-valley sides when the glaciers melt away. The river draining out of one of these lakes flows across the barrier at its lowest point and by erosion gradually cuts a trench through it. In time this becomes deep enough to drain the whole of the lake away. This has happened in many places and the flat, silted floors of Langdale and Kentmere (Figs. 133 and 138) are only examples. The river cannot, of course, cut the trench down below sea-level, so that a lake such as Loch Ness will never be completely drained in this way.

Rock hollows and steps

Besides barriers which result from points of reduced glacial erosion, it is possible to have the reverse effect—reaches of increased erosion. This particularly occurs when two glaciers unite without much widening of the valley. Increased thickness then results in a **rock hollow** or **rock basin** being cut and this is the case with many of the **finger lakes** in glaciated mountain regions.

Over-deepening of this kind produced the hollow that is the northern portion of Windermere where the glaciers from Langdale, Rydal, Stock Gill and Scandale joined together (Fig. 141). The shallowing at Bowness was caused by the glacier dividing into three as shown on the map, and the southern hollow occurred where the glacier from Hawkshead added its weight to the remaining portion of the main Windermere glacier.

The existence of a rock hollow almost automatically implies the existence of a rock barrier at the down-valley end.

There is one further variation in the long-profile of a single glacier, and this is a 'rock step'. This is a sudden deepening of the floor without a barrier up- or down-valley of it. It can occur whenever increased erosion is continued for a considerable distance down-valley.

Hanging valleys

'Hanging valleys' are related to rock steps. A hanging valley is formed when a weak glacier joins a strongly eroding one. In that case, the floor of the first glacier is not deepened so far as is the second. Although nothing is visible when the ice is present, once it melts away, we find the two valley

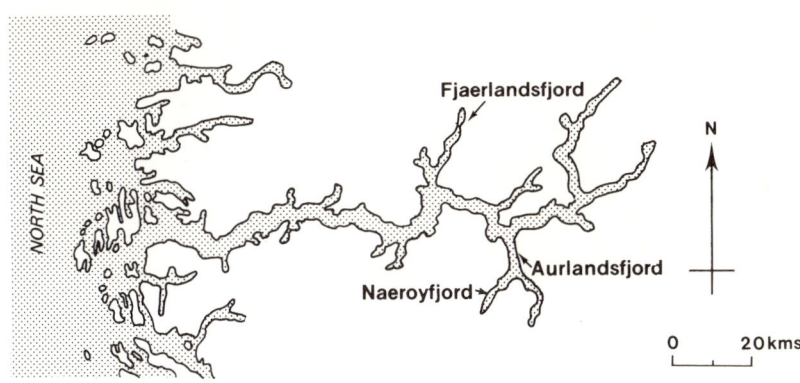

Fig. 143 The Sognefjord, drowned glaciated valleys

floors join one another at different levels. The one with the higher floor is called a hanging valley.

Fig. 142 shows a hanging valley near Geiteryggen (pronounced: *yett-er-ig-n*), east of Aurlandsfjord (Fig. 143). The floor of the main valley lies across the bottom of the picture and the tributary valley comes in at a much higher level. The modern river, which has taken the place of the glaciers that used to occupy this area, now cascades from the hanging valley and is cutting a groove down the slope. Many British waterfalls occur at hanging-valley junctions. Lodore Falls, near Keswick, is an example.

Crevasses

These irregularities in the slope of the rock floor and also in the width of the valley cause great stresses and strains in the ice. This is especially the case in the upper, brittle layers. Whenever there is a tension, the ice cracks open and crevasses are formed. Figs. 136 and 137 show the surface of a glacier with a large number of crevasses. They are both

Fig. 142 A hanging valley

93

Fig. 144 Deep crevasses on the Suphelle glacier, Norway

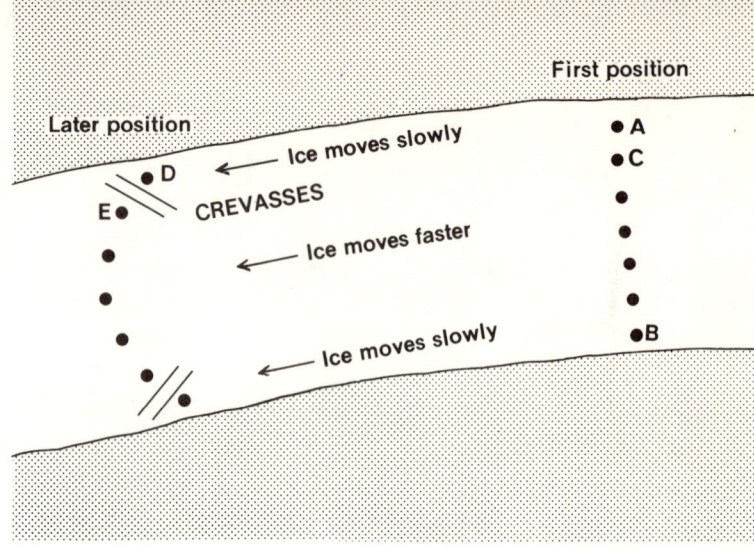

Fig. 145 The centre of a glacier moves faster than the sides

here approaching a steeper part of their valleys and as they are starting to move faster, the extra length has to be made up by air space.

Fig. 144 gives an idea of the size of crevasses. This photograph was taken in the summer when a certain amount of thaw was occurring and so the square-cut corners of the cracks had become rounded off.

Crevasses nearly always occur because the ice is under tension, due to an increase in size in some direction. Cracks make their appearance when a glacier rounds a corner. They are also found at the sides, even when it is moving straight. If a row of stones is placed in a straight line across the surface of a glacier from A to B as in Fig. 145, they are all found, say, a month later to have travelled down-valley, but the side ones have gone a shorter distance than those at the centre, where there is less friction.

Because of this, the distance from D to E is considerably greater than the original distance A to C between the same two stones. The ice cannot withstand this stretching and so crevasses appear across the line DE. Notice that the lengthening is always at right-angles to the direction of the crevasses. This type of crevasse is seen clearly at the foot of Fig. 146.

As conditions change, crevasses very often close up and perhaps new ones open. The pattern is continually altering. This adds to the excitement of crossing a glacier—it is never the same as when you came before. The climbers seen in Fig. 144 are roped together for safety. It is very risky to walk on a glacier after a recent fall of snow. Then some of the crevasses are hidden under the white blanket, as seen in Fig. 146, and it is easy to fall through into the unsuspected cavities beneath. The crevasses you cannot see are the dangerous ones.

If the valley becomes very steep, the ice breaks into separate pieces, and we have an **ice-fall**.

Fig. 146 Recent snow covers part of Kongsnut glacier, Finse, Norway

Fig. 149 shows Fjaerlandsfjord, viewed from 1500 metres up the mountains to the north. Below in the foreground is a glacier on the left, a moraine across the middle, and on the right a small lake trapped by the ice.

The fjords in Scotland are not quite so dramatic as in Norway, for the Scottish mountains do not rise to such heights and the glaciation was not so intense.

These fjords are exactly the same as the glacial valleys we have already been studying, except that their floors happen to be beneath sea-level right to their mouths and so they have become drowned by the sea.

Fig. 147 Milford Sound, New Zealand   (*Aerofilms Ltd.*)

Fjords

Most coasts in mountainous districts that have been glaciated are famous for their fjords. The west coast of Scotland has fjords. Those of Norway, Alaska and British Columbia are all well known. In the southern hemisphere examples are to be found in southern Chile and in South Island, New Zealand. (Fig. 147 shows Milford Sound, on the west coast of that country.) Iceland, Greenland and most Arctic and Antarctic islands have fjord coasts also.

An accurately drawn profile across Aurlandsfjord (Sognefjord, Fig. 143) is shown in Fig. 148. This reveals the upper limit to which the thickness of the glacier reached. It was at 1500 m above the true valley floor. The greatest depth of Sognefjord itself is just 1220 m below sea-level and at the same point it is clear that the ice top of the glacier reached to about 850 m. This gives a glacial-cut trough nearly 2100 m in depth.

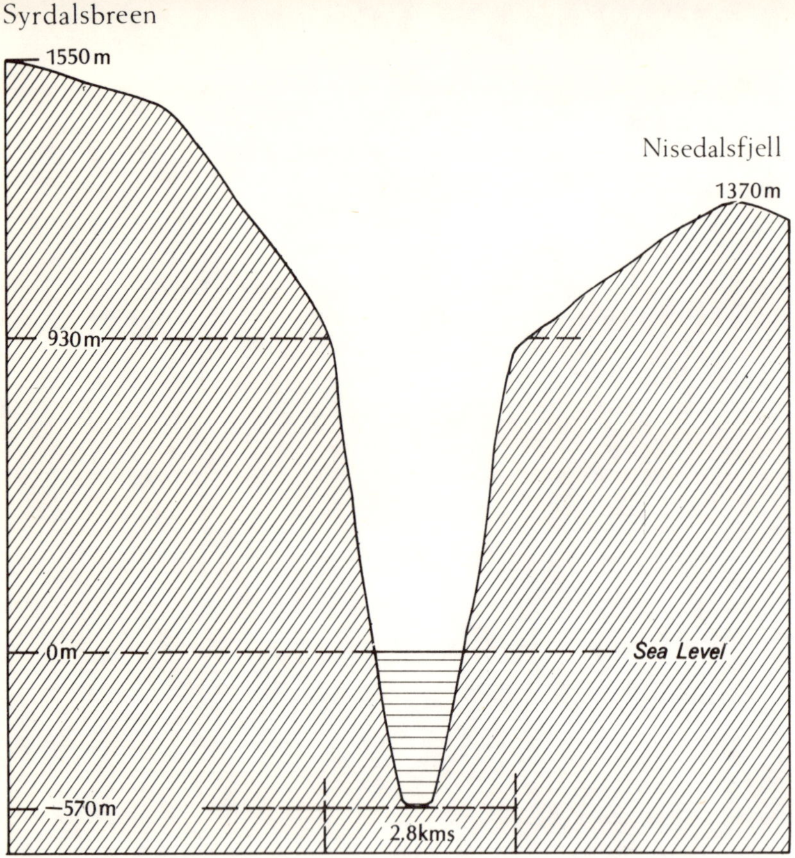

Syrdalsbreen

— 1550 m

Nisedalsfjell

1370 m

— 930 m

— 0 m   Sea Level

— −570 m

2.8 kms

Fig. 148 Profile across a fjord

Fig. 149 Fjaerlandsfjord seen from above

It is possible that the original pattern of these valleys, which very often is remarkably angular, may have been caused by geological reasons. Perhaps cracks or faults in the rocks encouraged pre-glacial rivers to make valleys in these directions. Then when the ice came, the rivers were replaced by glaciers in the same pattern.

The glaciers deepened the valleys so much that for great distances the floors now lie far below the present-day sea-level. But the landward end of the fjord is not generally the head of the glacial valley. There is a normal U-shaped valley extending beyond the end of most fjords. During glaciation, ice alone occupied these valleys, and the sea flooded them so far when the glaciers melted.

Most fjords have the usual 'down-at-heel' profile, and they are consequently shallower near their mouths than farther inland. This is described as having a 'shallow threshold', and will be considered more fully (see page 106).

Lateral moraines

A river can only move stones that fall into it if they are sufficiently small and the water is moving sufficiently fast.

96

The conditions are quite different with a glacier. Any rock, however large, that is broken off the mountain-side, probably by freeze-thaw, and falls on to the ice is carried along with it.

In the kind of climate that produces glaciers, freeze-thaw is generally very active, and so the sides of a glacier are most often covered with heaps of shattered boulders. This material is called **lateral moraine**. Fig. 137 shows a line of dark boulders at the left edge of the glacier. This is the lateral moraine. The same is seen on the far side of the tributary glacier in Fig. 150. When the ice eventually melts completely away, the moraine forms a heap along the side of the glaciated valley.

It usually happens that the screes, formed by the valley-wall collapse that occurs when the ice melts, cover the lateral moraines completely, so that they are not often seen.

Fig. 151 Medial moraine at the snout of Kongsnut glacier, Finse

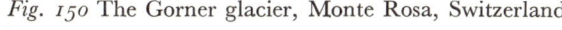

Fig. 150 The Gorner glacier, Monte Rosa, Switzerland

Medial moraines

When two glaciers join one another, they continue on their way side by side along the single valley they now occupy. Practically no mixing takes place. In this way a middle or **medial moraine** is produced by the union of two of the laterals. The medial moraine appears as a ridge of boulders along the surface of the united glacier and is seen as a grey line in the middle of the ice in Fig. 137. There are several medial moraines on Fig. 150. One is in the middle of the tributary glacier and another is formed from the laterals where the glaciers meet. Fig. 151 shows a medial moraine at the snout of a glacier coming from the Hardanger ice-cap.

These moraines are not only composed of rocks that have fallen to the top of the ice. Besides this, there is the broken material between the side of the glacier and the valley wall, the result of erosion (see Fig. 152). Lateral moraines, therefore, generally extend down the full depth of the

97

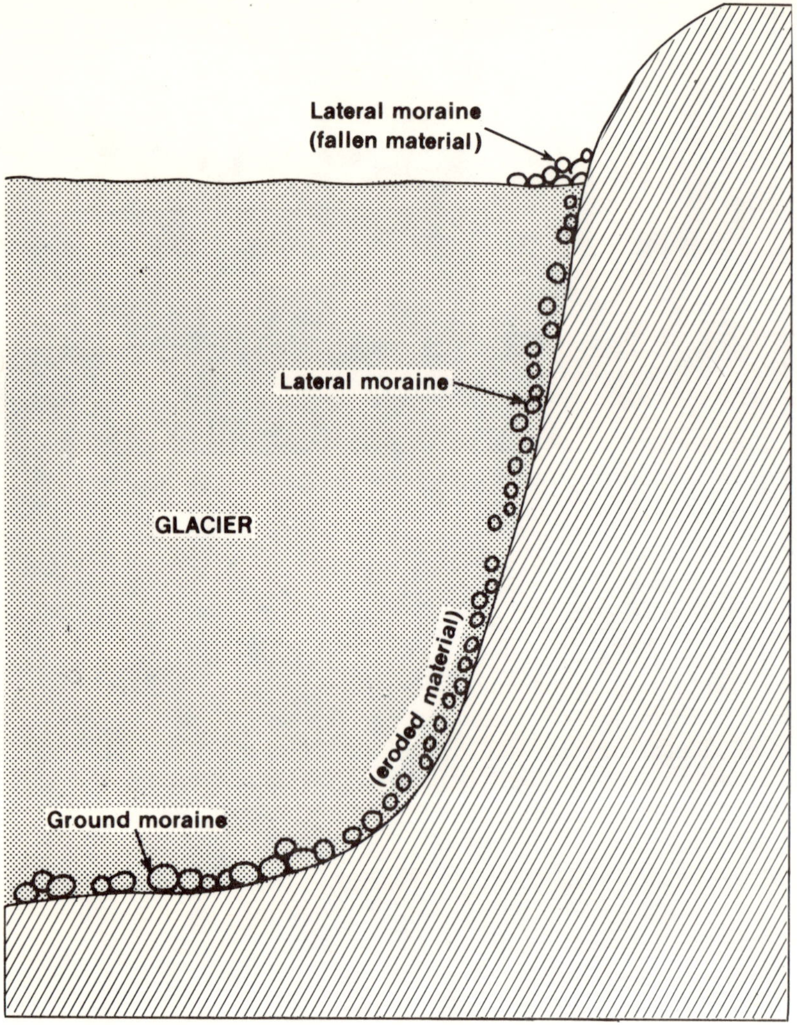

Fig. 153 A glacier with much clay and many boulders on its surface

**Lateral moraine
(fallen material)**

Lateral moraine

GLACIER

(eroded material)

Ground moraine

Fig. 152 Lateral moraine

glacier, and when a medial is formed it, too, generally has considerable depth within the ice.

Fig. 153 shows how much material a glacier may carry. The grey surface of the ice is a layer of finely ground rock and many boulders are seen in the foreground. The crevasses obviously let a considerable amount of rock fall into the interior of the glacier, and so the debris becomes embedded in the midst of the ice as the crevasses close again.

Ground moraine—ice-smoothed rock

As it moves over its rock bed, the glacier plucks, grinds and drags pieces of rock away. Fig. 154 shows how vertical layers of rock were bent over by the ice moving from left to right across the top surface. These rocks, on the eastern side of Windermere, were just about to be taken along in the bottom of the ice at the moment when it stopped moving, at the end of the Ice Ages.

98

Fig. 154 Vertical layers of rock overturned by Windermere glacier

Fig. 156 Ice-smoothed rock at Bowness, near Windermere

Fig. 155 Ice scratches in rock on Ingleborough, Yorkshire. The hammer gives the size.

Fig. 157 '*Roche moutonnée*' in Llanberis Pass, Snowdonia

Some of the plucked rocks remain embedded in the bottom of the ice and often partly project. Sharp points on them produce scratches or striations or **striae** on the surface of the solid rock floor. These lines are most often only half a centimetre or so in depth, and in Fig. 155 the faint white lines show that ice moved either from left to right or in the reverse direction.

Besides scratching it, the glacier smooths the rock and produces the kind of surface shown in Fig. 156. This is a feature seen very often in all glaciated areas. The dark lines running across the rock are not striations, but the result of later weathering. Grooves like these are very often mistaken for striations, which are by no means common.

Plucking and smoothing gives rise to the landform known as a **roche moutonnée**. Fig. 157 shows this in the Llanberis Pass in North Wales, and the size can be judged by the wall in the foreground. The ice moved from left to right, smoothed the up- and plucked the down-valley sides.

Very often a heap of boulders of all sizes accumulates on the lee side of a **roche moutonnée**, probably during the last stages of glaciation, when the ice is less active and plucking has ceased. This produces the upstanding, solid, ice-smoothed rock, with the long gentle incline of loose material, as seen in Fig. 158. This is known as **crag and tail**, and the details of their formation are very closely associated with drumlins, which will be described later (page 116).

Fig. 158 The crag and tail effect

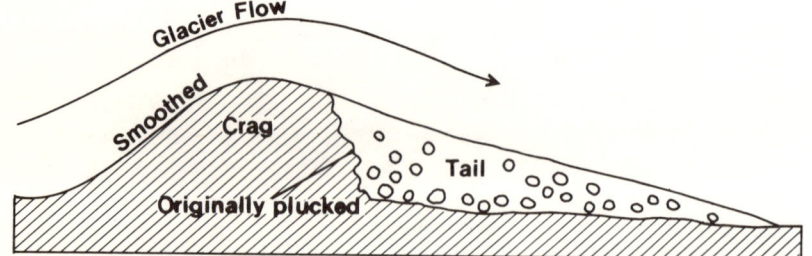

14   The terminus of a glacier

As the glacier slowly comes down from the high mountain levels, it moves into warmer regions and thaw commences. It is not easy for the surface of snow or ice to melt.

Melting ice

It takes about as much heat to melt ice as it does to boil the same weight of cold tap-water. This heat does not alter the temperature and it is necessary to do the actual melting. It is called 'latent heat'. It is very fortunate that so large a quantity is required, for it slows down the rate at which snow or ice melts. As it is, rivers that are fed by meltwater from glaciers are always in full spate during the summer. If ice and snow melted more readily, very serious floods would result in the valleys below.

Snow and ice also melt slowly for a second, quite different, reason. Radiant heat from the sun finds it difficult to get into the ice on which it shines. We find snow and ice so dazzlingly bright because they reflect most of the sunlight that shines down on their surface. In addition to this, they reflect about three-quarters of the arriving radiant sun-heat and absorb only the remaining one-quarter.

When we walk on a glacier, we can be quite warm whilst the ice shows no signs of melting, even on a sunny day. We are generally wearing dark-coloured clothing and so absorb the radiant heat from the sun and are warmed by it. In addition we receive some of the sun-heat reflected from the glacier. We are, in a way, warmed twice.

The same effect occurs with the rocks on either side of the glacier or any boulder that may be resting on it. The rock absorbs the heat and is warmed. It then re-radiates the heat, but this time with a considerably longer wave-length. This is called 'black' radiant heat, since the object that is

Fig. 159 Ice thaws away from the rock

Fig. 160 The glacier surface is low at the sides

radiating it is not actually glowing. You can feel this kind of heat by holding your hand fairly near an electric fire and switching it on. You can detect the black heat long before the element glows.

Snow and ice can absorb black heat, and be warmed and so melted by it. Fig. 159 shows the ice thawed away for more than 20 cms distance from a large boulder. It was melted by the black heat from the rock.

The side of a glacier

Fig. 160 is of the edge of the Suphelle glacier which we have already seen in general in Fig. 136. The climber gives the scale. He is walking on ice. On his left is the rock side of the valley. Beyond him and on his right everything is ice. The skyline is the general level of the glacier, and one always has to come down quite a steep ice slope (on the right) when approaching the edge. Fig. 161 makes this clearer and shows how the re-radiated heat from the rock sides melts the ice nearby. A glacier always first melts at the sides.

When you walk on a glacier, after descending this slope to the edge, it is often still quite difficult to find a way off the ice, because it is also melted underneath at the edge itself.

This under-melting is a fact that has always to be borne in mind when walking on snow or ice. The ice may have melted beneath, even well away from the edge, and be tunnelled. If the roof is thin, this could give way under your weight and be very dangerous. Fig. 162 shows places where the roof of a tunnel has collapsed in several places in this manner.

These tunnels often appear at the snout or end of the glacier, as is seen in Fig. 163. The people on the left give the size. Meltwater is pouring out from this tunnel, the roof is becoming rather thin and unsupported, and a crevasse is already forming as the ice is about to collapse.

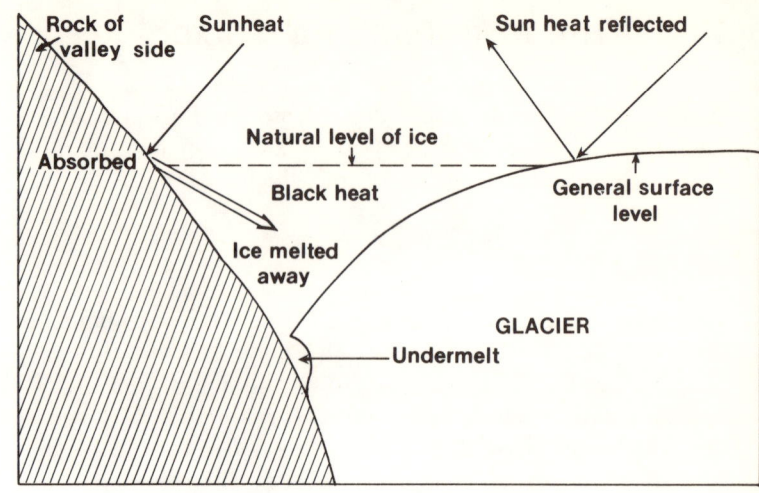

Fig. 161 A glacier melts faster at the edge

Fig. 162 Part of the glacier surface has collapsed into a tunnel in the ice

Fig. 163 An under-ice tunnel ends at the snout of Boyum glacier, Norway

Fig. 164 The snout of Kongsnut glacier

The glacier snout

The snout or terminus of a glacier is located where the rate of arrival of ice equals the rate of thaw. From the point where melting exceeded accumulation, the glacier has become smaller in volume. Eventually there is a quite definite place where the whole of the remaining ice melts. Fig. 164 shows the termination of Kongsnut glacier, which comes from the Hardanger snowfield. The glacier occupies the whole width between the two mountains and Fig. 165 explains the details of the picture. The ice thins out until it has all melted away.

Blaaisen (pronounced: *blah-eess-en*), the Blue Ice glacier, also at Finse, comes from a snowfield, becomes a glacier between mountain-walls and then moves beyond the mountains on to a wide, flat area. Here it expands out into a great semi-circle of ice and is what is called a **piedmont glacier**. Fig. 166 shows deep longitudinal crevasses formed because of the increase in width as it spreads. In the foreground there is meltwater and a small quantity of moraine.

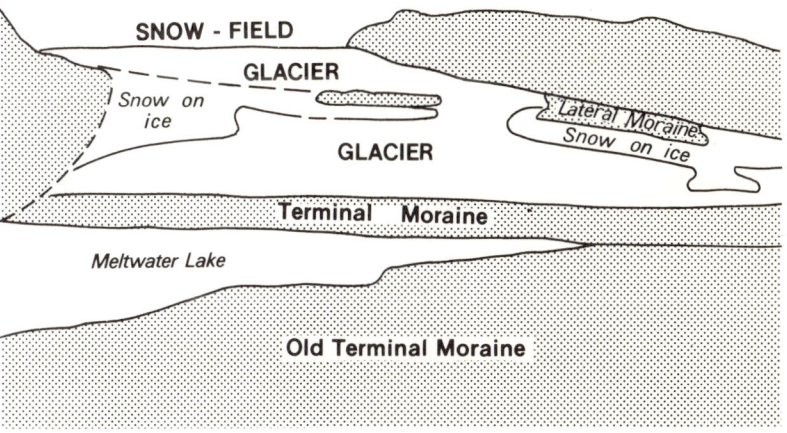

Fig. 165 Key diagram to Fig. 164

Fig. 166 The crevassed snout of a piedmont glacier

Fig. 167 Moraine-covered glacier snout

The near view of part of the snout of another glacier shows how much debris may be brought down. In this photograph (Fig. 167) almost all the ice is completely covered by finely ground-up rock and by boulders of all sizes. There is also the mouth of a tunnel in the ice.

At the snout, all the morainic material the glacier was carrying falls to the ground. The meltwater streams are able to remove some by ordinary river processes and this is dealt with later on in this chapter. The remainder of the debris remains in great heaps as **terminal moraines**.

Terminal moraines

Examples of a terminal moraine have already been noticed in Fig. 164. This shows a large area of moraine, which has been deposited annually during the last twenty years, whilst the glacier has been 'retreating', that is, whilst the position of the snout has gradually moved towards the mountains.

The ice here is now, on the whole, melting just a little faster than fresh ice arrives, and so the net loss shows itself by the glacier slowly becoming shorter. If, for example, the ice moves forwards one metre a week and if a length of 1.2 m melts off the end in the same time, the position of the snout will move back 0.2 m. Notice carefully that the ice itself does not retreat; only the *position* of the snout does so.

Fig. 168 shows Blaaisen glacier (see also Fig. 166) about one kilometre away from the snout. The foreground consists of moraine which has been deposited only recently, perhaps within the last twenty years. It is still quite fresh and scarcely any vegetation has yet taken root upon it. When a glacier is retreating, a series of moraines is built up, one behind the other.

This same picture gives a good idea of the glacier as a whole, moving in from between the rock outcrops on the two sides.

Fig. 169 shows the appearance of a terminal moraine long after the glacier has completely melted away. It is at Trins, south of Innsbruck. The glacier moved from right to left and the moraine marks the limit reached by the ice during a late stage of the glaciation.

The glacier in the Windermere valley reached the Irish Sea for a long period, but as it gradually decayed, when the climate became warmer, the snout slowly moved up-valley. It took many years for the glacier to shorten so much that it eventually ceased to exist, and it would be possible for terminal moraines to be found in any position along the whole length of the valley. However, main accumulations of debris are found at points where the snout stood for some years and material had more time to collect. The down-valley end of Windermere itself is one such position, and Fig. 170 shows a terminal moraine stretching across the southern end of the lake like a great embankment of stones of all sizes, now grassed over.

Fig. 169 Trins terminal moraine, Austrian Tirol

Fig. 170 The terminal moraine at the south end of Windermere

Fig. 168 A retreating glacier leaves a great spread of terminal moraine

Tidal glaciers

Most glaciers terminate before they reach low-lying ground and the coast. In sufficiently cold climates, however, they may extend as far as the sea. These are called tidal glaciers, and generally the snout is in the form of a cliff of ice. The Dawson Lambton glacier on the Caird coast to the south of the Weddell sea, Antarctica, is one of this type (Fig. 171). The photographer was over the crevassed snout and sections of it are breaking off, or **calving**, and floating out to sea as icebergs (see page 114).

In the case of tidal glaciers the debris eventually falls to the sea floor and no normal terminal moraine is formed.

Although they have not melted completely away, tidal glaciers have generally thinned considerably by the time they are in contact with the water. Because of the fact that ice is larger than the same weight of water, it is lighter and

Fig. 171 Icebergs breaking off the snout of a tidal glacier
(*Official U.S. Navy Photograph*)

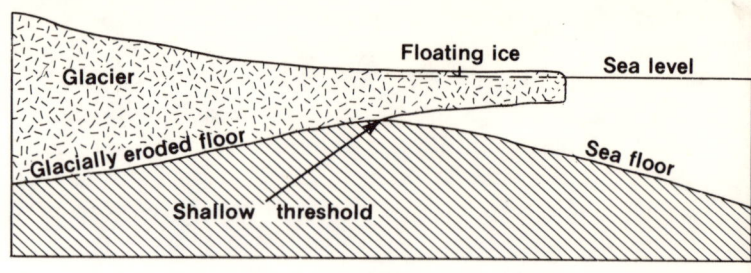

Fig. 172 A fjord has a shallow threshold

therefore floats. One-twelfth of its volume is above water level in fresh water, or about one-ninth in sea water. This means that a glacier, on entering the sea, will not float off the bottom until the depth of the water is eight-ninths the thickness of the ice. A glacier 270 m thick will just float in water 240 m deep, with 30 m of ice projecting. These figures vary a little with different glaciers and bergs, because the density of glacier ice is not always quite the same, depending on whether or not all the air has been driven out of it.

The usual down-at-heel effect of glacial valleys is found in fjords, so that the present water depths become less as we approach the open sea. At the place where the ice floated off the valley floor, glacial erosion ceased. There is thus a point near the mouth where the fjord is least deep, and this is known as the 'shallow threshold' (see Fig. 172).

All fjords have shallow thresholds and they vary in depth from fjord to fjord. Each one was formed independently and its level results from the thickness of its own glacier. Fig. 173 shows several of the fjords on the west coast of Scotland south of Skye. All have irregular floors and shallow thresholds. Loch Hourn has its at 90 m below sea-level although shortly up-valley it is as deep as 180 m.

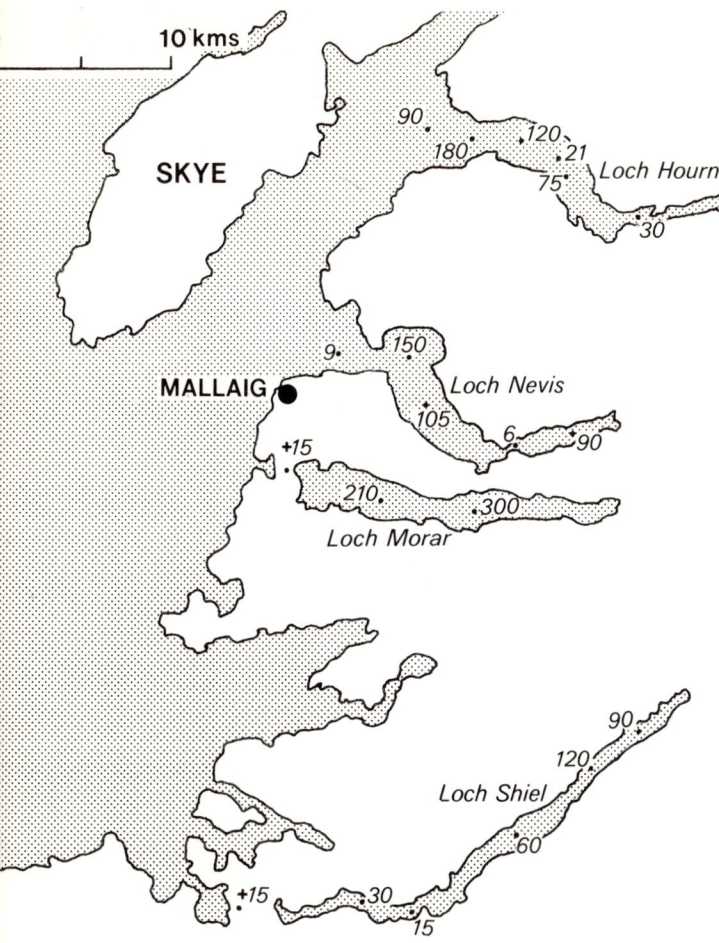

Fig. 173 Fjords on the west coast of Scotland

Loch Nevis has only 9 m of water at its mouth with 150 m farther in. Loch Morar has its threshold more than 15 m above the present sea-level with depths as low as minus 300 m within what has naturally become a lake.

Glacial meltwater

The snout of a glacier is the place where the load ceases to be moved by ice and must continue by water-transport if it is to continue at all. Terminal moraines are composed of the larger boulders and of smaller ones that have become jammed against them. The meltwater has so far been unable to move them. Because much of the melting occurs at the sides of glaciers, streams of water flow along the edges of the valley between the rock and the ice. They often remove lateral moraines and prevent the formation of terminal moraines near the valley-sides. Most terminal moraines therefore have gaps at either end, as well as one or two in the middle.

Kames

Since most snouts have retreated up-valley during recent years, it is very common to find abandoned terminal moraines down-valley of the present terminus. Sometimes they have no gaps and do block the whole width of the valley. Then a lake accumulates between them and the existing snout. The meltwater streams pour into the lake.

As they do so, their speed is slackened and they deposit most of the load they are carrying. Deltas, called **kames**, are built (see Fig. 174).

The sand and gravel of which they are composed is in layers, as are most stream-lain deposits. Some of the layers are horizontal, but others, which formed the front face of the delta, are quite steeply inclined. Fig. 175 shows the quarried face of a large kame at Carnforth, north of

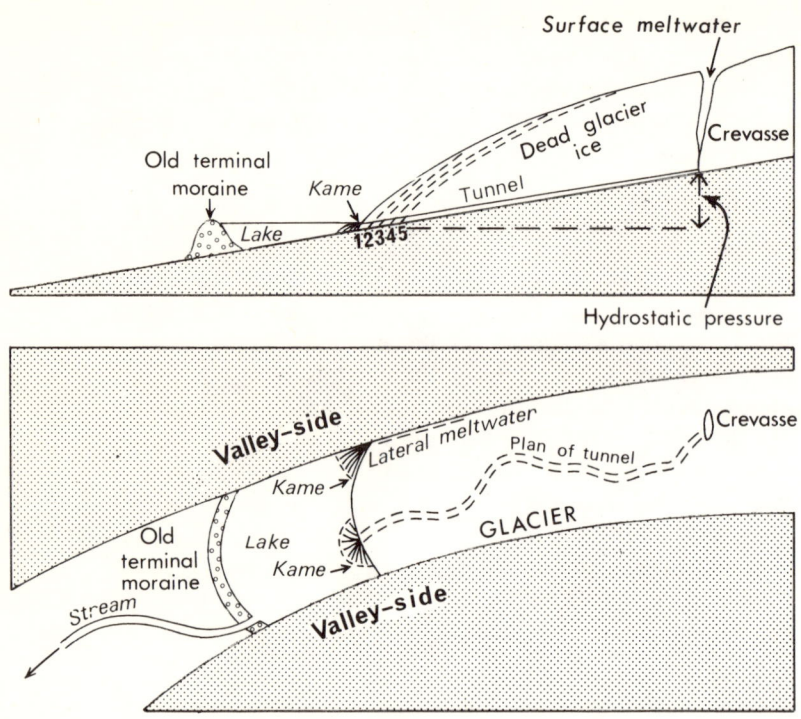

Fig. 174 Formation of kames and eskers

Lancaster. The exposed face is 24 m in height. Fig. 176 shows another kame, this time near Trim, County Meath, Ireland. Notice the steeply inclined beds.

Kames may also be deposited at the mouths of glacial tunnels. Whilst a glacier is decaying as the climate becomes warmer, a stage is reached when the ice is more or less stagnant. This is called 'dead ice'. As usual, there are crevasses. Meltwater from the surface falls down and in time thaws out a tunnel for itself through the ice that it meets. Figs. 163 and 167 have already shown examples.

If the tunnel becomes full of water to the roof, considerable pressure is set up because the beginning of the tunnel (see Fig. 174) is higher than the mouth. The water is forced along the tunnel by this pressure and travels much faster than it would with the same gradient in the open air as an ordinary river. This forced flow is exactly the same as the forced flow of tap-water through the town's pipes, where the height of the reservoir provides the pressure.

Fig. 175 A section in a kame in north Lancashire

Fig. 176 Steeply inclined deposits in a kame

Eskers

Besides mounds of these kinds, another feature is found in the same localities. Fig. 177 shows a ridge of sand and gravel snaking across the fields, with occasional higher and broader parts. The two men in the distance are standing on one of these knobs. This kind of feature is known as a **beaded esker**. Fig. 178 shows an esker half-drowned in Strangford Lough, south of Belfast. The enlarged portion at the right-hand end is a kame.

These eskers, like kames, are composed of sand and gravel deposited more or less in layers. They often are the result of the under-ice tunnels becoming half choked with material the stream is unable to carry any farther. The esker is thus formed along the length of the tunnel behind the kame. When the glacier melts away, it is left in the shape of the tunnel's path (see Fig. 174).

Other eskers are elongated kames. If the glacier decayed quickly to positions 1, 2, 3, 4, 5, etc. (see Fig. 174), there

Fig. 177 A beaded esker at Collessie, Fife

Moving at such high speed within the tunnel, the water can carry boulders that it would not normally be able to move. These boulders in time come out of the mouth of the tunnel at the glacier snout. Once in the open and also able to spread, the water moves much more slowly and so drops most of its load.

A third type of kame is constructed when meltwater tumbles down a crevasse, which is wide enough at the bottom to let water through, probably into an ice-tunnel, but sufficiently narrow to trap most of the debris that is washed into it. When the ice eventually melts, this heap of material is dropped to the ground as a somewhat disorderly heap of gravel.

Sometimes a number of kames, of any type, are formed so near one another that they merge and produce what is called a **kame terrace**.

Fig. 178 An esker and kame half-drowned by the sea

would be no time to form more than a small delta at these points. This would produce the embankment-like mound, and whenever the decay slowed down for a time a larger amount of debris would be deposited. This would form one of the beads on the esker.

There is quite a variety of other kinds of meltwater deposits, but kames and eskers are the most important. Sometimes the material is sand and gravel mixed; sometimes it is almost pure sand. Generally it varies from layer to layer—a reflection of the speed of the water-flow that deposited it. Gravel indicates a flow fast enough for the current to carry the sand farther on, and it is generally laid down during the summer, when the river is in spate, fed by the melting ice. In the spring and autumn, there is less melting, the outflowing streams move more slowly, and sand is deposited.

Clay nearly always has been carried right away, and this is what often makes these deposits so valuable as concrete aggregate, in which the presence of clay would be a great disadvantage.

15   Sheet Ice

There are two distinct types of ice sheet. One type is formed on lowland plains due to separate glaciers from the surrounding mountains joining together and forming one more or less continuous cover. Other ice sheets come into existence direct from the local snowfall. These are generally on plateaux and high mountain areas.

Upland ice caps

The great ice cap of Greenland is an example of this second type (see Fig. 179). It covers more than three-quarters of the whole island and has an area of nearly two million square kilometres which is more than eleven times the area of England and Wales. It is more than 3 km thick in the deepest part, which is rather to the east of the centre of the island, and it seems that the rock surface in much of these inner parts lies below sea-level, perhaps because the Earth's crust has sagged under the weight of this huge mass of ice.

At the edges, the ice is thinner and mountain summits often project up above it. True glaciers are formed, and as they move down steeper slopes in narrower paths, they travel rather more rapidly.

Fig. 180 (photographed in August), shows the largest ice cap still in existence in continental Europe. It is nearly 100 km long and up to 32 km wide. It gives birth to a large number of glaciers, of which the Suphelle (see Fig. 136) is one. This ice cap is called the Jostedal (pronounced: *yost-e-dahl*) and is north of the Sognefjord. It is about 2300 m high in the centre, but probably less than 600 m of this is ice.

Fig. 181 shows the Vatnajökull in Iceland. The ice-surface contours show that it rises to more than 2000 metres on what appears to be a mountainous area. The highest

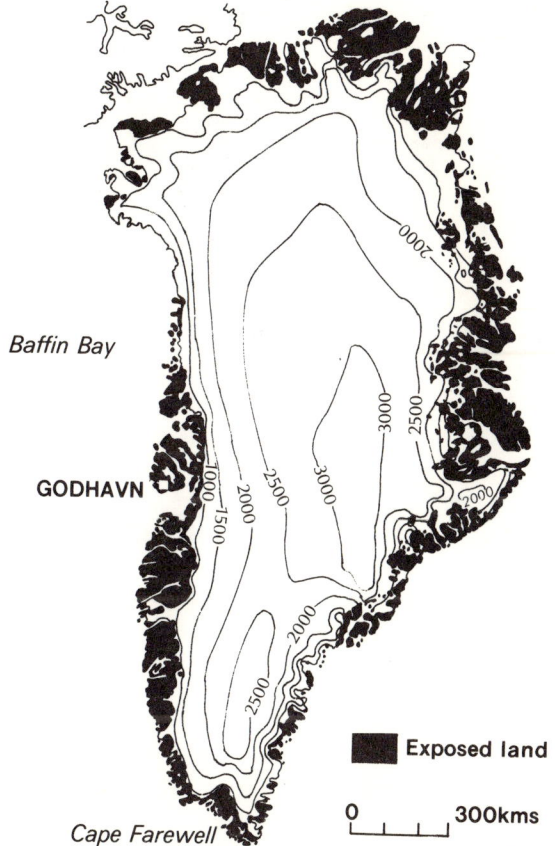

Fig. 179 Greenland is mostly covered by an ice sheet

Fig. 180 Jostedalsbreen, the largest ice sheet in continental Europe

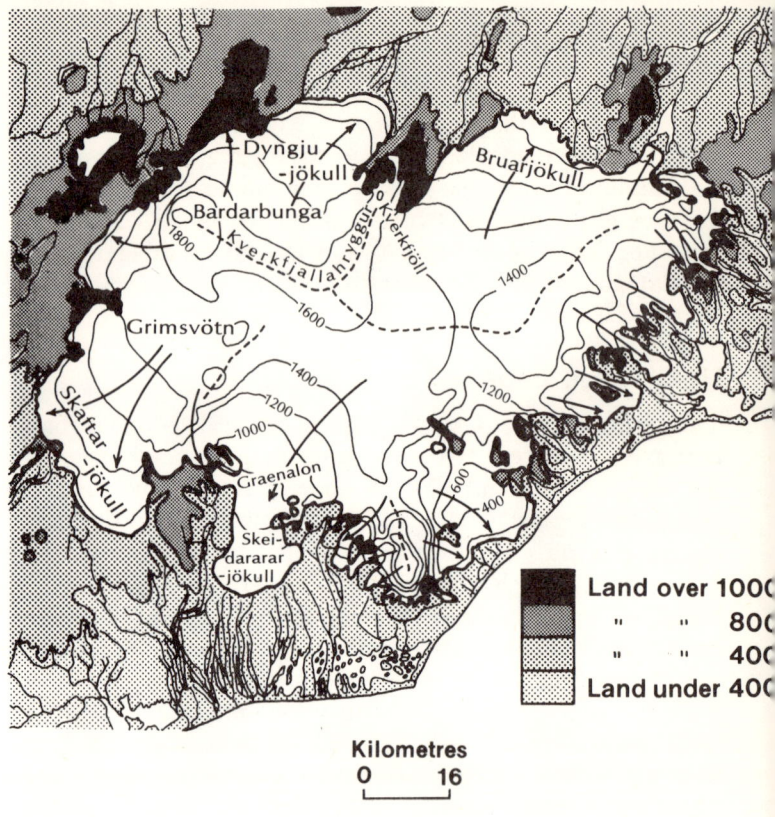

Land over 1000
   "   "   800
   "   "   400
Land under 400

Kilometres
0   16

Fig. 181 Vatnajökull in southern Iceland

extensive ice area is a kind of broad ridge, linking Bardar-bunga with Kverkfjöll. The ice descends outwards from this area and from another, connected, high area above 1400 metres at the eastern end of the field. This probably masks a high land area beneath. Tiny **nunataks**, or exposed peaks of rock, appear above the ice at Grimsvötn, and these are a clear indication of mountains almost entirely enveloped. Something like thirteen main glaciers, and many small ones, flow from the one ice sheet.

One or two of the glaciers, such as Skeidararjökull and Skaftarjökull, extend beyond the limits of the mountains and become piedmont glaciers. A pro-glacial lake, Grae-nalon, lies in a shallow rock trough between two blocks of ice.

In Britain many of the more level upland areas, such as some of the Pennine Moors and the Meigneint Moors, in

North Wales south-east of Snowdonia (see Fig. 182), had their own small ice caps during the Ice Ages, and many of the mountainous districts must have looked very much the same as Fig. 180 at that time.

The largest present-day ice-covered area is the Antarctic (see Fig. 183), where the area is something like thirteen million square kilometres. It used to be thought that most of Antarctica was a continent, but recent surveys have thrown some doubt on this, and it is now considered that the general level of the rock surface is largely below the level of the open ocean, and that the ice is so thick that it rests directly on this sea floor. The various mountain ranges that project through the ice may in some case be islands, rather than the higher parts of what would be continuous land area if all the ice melted.

Fig. 182 High moorland south-west of Snowdonia

Fig. 183 Theron Mountains appearing like nunataks above the Antarctic ice sheet (*Norsk Polarinstitutt*)

Floating ice

When either a glacier or part of an ice sheet reaches the sea without melting entirely, it rides on the sea floor until there is sufficient depth of water to float it. This has already been explained in connection with tidal glaciers, and exactly the same applies when ice sheets reach the ocean. The shelf ice in Ross Sea and in Weddell Sea provides examples of this on a large scale. The Ross Ice Shelf has an area of about 500 000 square kilometres. The seaward part has come off the rock floor and floats. It continues to move slowly northwards, pushed by the ice behind it, always becoming thinner and thinner as it gradually melts away. When it is only a hundred metres or so thick, pieces very often break off from the front edge and float away as icebergs.

A berg is always a much more massive object than it appears, for we can only see the one-ninth part that is above the water level (see Fig. 184). The bergs drift with the ocean current and often travel hundreds of kilometres in the cold, polar water before they melt away entirely.

Fig. 184 Iceberg and thick pack ice in the Weddell Sea (*Aerofilms Ltd.*)

Bergs are always formed in this way, and should not be confused with 'ice floes', which are much thinner pieces of ice, formed by the surface of the sea itself freezing. Salt water requires a lower temperature than fresh to freeze it, but the climate is quite cold enough to do this in polar regions.

Floes often break up into slabs sometimes quite small, but often a square kilometre or more in area. This is called 'pack ice' (see Fig. 184). Most atlases contain maps that show the limits reached by pack ice, and in the Atlantic in the spring it reaches as far south as Nova Scotia and Newfoundland on the west. Shipping routes between Europe and United States are moved southwards in the winter and spring, so as to avoid areas of ocean where ice is likely to occur and be a danger.

Floating ice has a much more northerly limit on the east, because of the warming effect of the Gulf Stream Drift.

Lowland ice sheets

When the area of ice was at its maximum during the Ice Ages, the glaciers coming from, say, the Lake District, joined together as they passed beyond the valleys (see Fig. 185). They filled the Irish Sea and forced all the water out of it. They covered the Lancashire coastal plain. As a great ice sheet, the material moved southwards, both along St. George's Channel and across the Cheshire-Shropshire plain.

The same kind of movement occurred on the eastern side of Britain. Scottish and Pennine glaciers moved eastwards towards the North Sea. Great masses of Scandinavian ice came into the same area and for at least part of the time the North Sea was filled with ice across its whole width. Boulders of Scandinavian rocks can be found in the morainic and outwash cliffs of north Norfolk.

Similar ice sheets covered northern Germany, north and central USSR, lowland Sweden, the whole of Denmark, and filled all the Baltic. Probably all Canada and the most northern of the United States were similarly overwhelmed by ice.

Indicator erratics

Erratics are boulders which have been moved by ice from their original position and later dropped, as the ice melted, in some new locality. They may have been moved a mere few hundred metres or for several hundred kilometres. Fig. 186 shows an erratic block of Silurian rock perched on a short column of limestone. This is one of a number of famous erratics at Norber on the south side of Ingleborough. The height of the pedestal indicates the thickness of limestone that has been weathered away from the remainder of the area since the erratic was deposited. The boulder is rather less than two metres in height.

Some rocks, mostly igneous ones, are unique in the sense

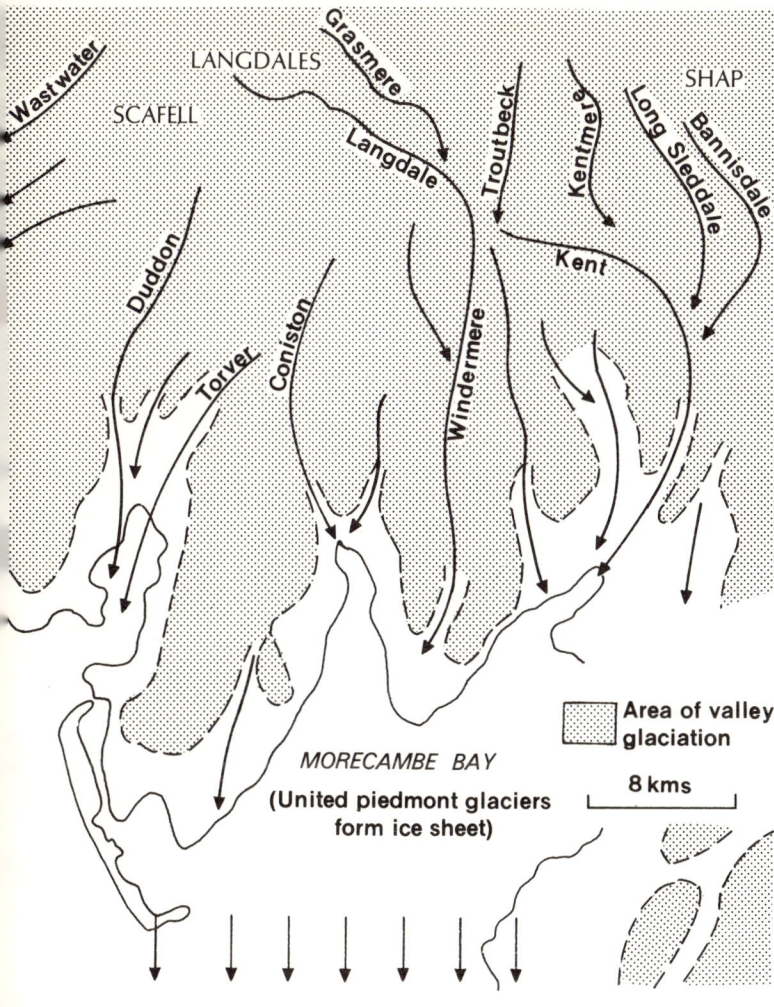

Fig. 185 Glaciers in north-west England

Labels on map: Wastwater, LANGDALES, SCAFELL, Grasmere, Langdale, Troutbeck, Kentmere, SHAP, Bannisdale, Long Sleddale, Kent, Duddon, Coniston, Torver, Windermere, MORECAMBE BAY (United piedmont glaciers form ice sheet)

Area of valley glaciation

8 kms

Fig. 186 An erratic of Silurian rock perched on limestone

that the particular variety is only to be found at one locality. For example, there is a special type of granite that only occurs on Ailsa Craig, a small island in the outer Clyde estuary. This rock is easily recognized by those who know it, and specimens have been found lying in the glacial debris, dropped when the ice melted, along almost the whole of the east coast of Ireland and the west coast of England and Wales from about Blackpool to Pembroke. Specimens have been found in the Cheshire plain.

Several other areas have their own unique rocks also. By tracing these indicator erratics, it is possible to discover the main directions followed by the moving ice sheets. Fig. 187 gives a simplified indication of these routes for the later glaciations. Although the ice moved generally southwards, it was often forced sideways, as happened across the northern Pennines.

Most of lowland Britain, north of a line through Hereford, Banbury and St. Albans, was covered by these ice sheets during the earlier glaciations. The later glaciations did not reach so far. Their limits are also marked on Fig. 187.

Drumlins

Besides a general smoothing of many of the irregularities on the pre-glacial rock surface, the ice bulldozed and dragged away almost the whole of the original soil and carried with it a great deal of broken rock in pieces of all sizes from silt and clay to boulders many metres in diameter.

One curious feature is found as the result of this. It is the **drumlin**, the Irish name for a small ridge. A drumlin is a smooth, oval-shaped mound up to 30 m or so in height and most often between one and two kilometres in length. Fig. 188 shows one at the side of the Duddon estuary, north of Barrow. Fig. 189 shows a collection half-drowned in Strangford Lough, Co. Down, and Fig. 190 shows the same from the ground.

They are formed underneath the ice. Whilst the sheet is slowly moving over the countryside, there is a layer of broken rock, **ground moraine**, between the ice and the solid rock floor. The filling of this sandwich, the broken material, has the choice of moving along with the ice or of remaining stationary with the solid rock. Which choice it accepts is controlled by the relative ease of movement—whether it is easier for the ice to slide over the broken rock, or for the broken rock to slide over the solid floor.

When there is a considerable amount of ground moraine, it often happens that there is less friction if the loose material remains more or less stationary on the ground. Other debris coming along then becomes caught up with what is already there and the great heap accumulates. It is streamlined, with its longer length along the line of ice movement and the ice sheet glides smoothly over it.

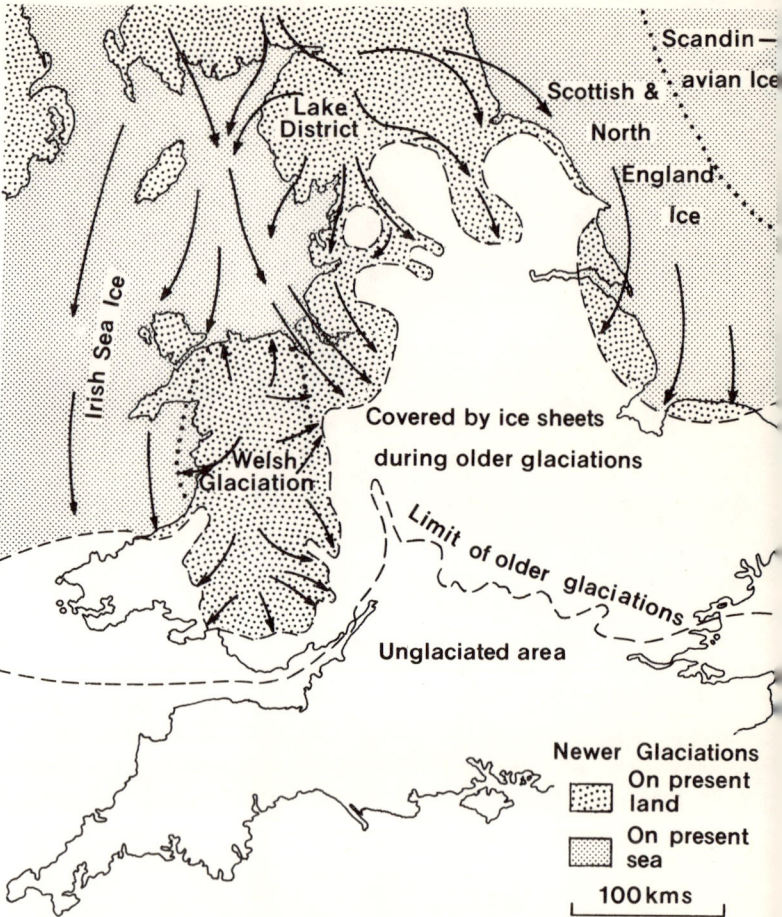

Fig. 187 The movements of ice in England and Wales

Fig. 188 A drumlin

Fig. 190 A drumlin on the western side of Strangford Lough

Fig. 189 Drumlins half-drowned in Strangford Lough

There are all varieties of drumlins, from those which consist entirely of morainic material, to those which are in reality roches moutonnées plastered over with a thin layer of ground moraine.

When the ice melts away, the drumlins are left as seen in the photographs. They occur on the plains, often in great clusters, such as in County Down and in Yorkshire to the west of Skipton (Fig. 191), where the ground is almost entirely covered. This group contributed to the alteration in the route taken by the river Ribble. Before the Ice Ages, it is thought to have flowed to the south-east and joined with the river Aire (Fig. 192), but the drumlins blocked this old route when the area melted out, and the Ribble had to find a new way to the sea. It tumbled over the area to the north-west of the drumlin group, cut a gorge for itself, and found older rivers that flowed to the Irish Sea.

Drumlins form fairly dry areas, but are often too hard to plough. If the ice sheet came from limestone country, the

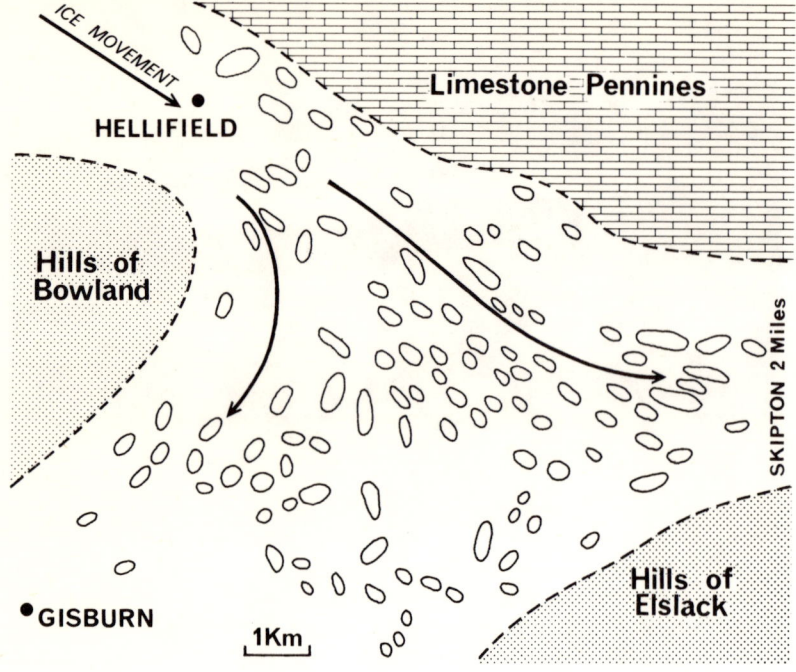

Fig. 191 A swarm of drumlins near Skipton, Yorkshire

in or on the sheet falls to the ground to form an uneven covering known as **till**. The same deposit is often called **boulder clay**, but quite commonly it contains very few boulders, and sometimes it is so sandy that it has scarcely any clay. These variations depend mainly on the kinds of rock that have supplied the material for the till, and on how far it is from the mountains.

As larger erratics are moved farther afield, they are ground ever smaller. At Lancaster many of the boulders in the till, which has mostly come from the Lake District, perhaps from about 25 km away, are a metre or more in diameter. Near Liverpool, boulders larger than 40 cm in diameter are rare. In Shropshire, erratics, still from the Lake District, are scarcely ever larger than cricket balls. So the size progressively decreases.

moraine is often cemented together, almost into a concrete. When drumlins occur in clusters the roads have to wind their way between them.

Drumlins are also found in the wider parts of glaciated valleys.

Till

When a glaciation comes to an end, the lowland ice-sheets, as well as the glaciers, cease moving and become dead ice. Eventually they melt away, and whatever debris lay under,

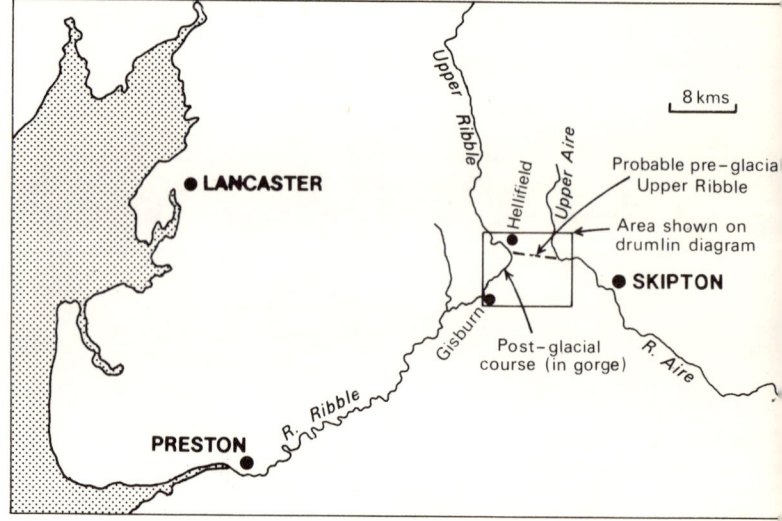

Fig. 192 River Ribble changed its route after the Ice Ages

118

Fig. 193 Till deposited on limestone on the south coast of the Isle of Man

Fig. 194 Farming is difficult in very stony till

The typical characteristic of till, by which it can be distinguished from other deposits, is its unsorted character (see Fig. 193). It shows no signs of being in layers, as it would if it had been water-deposited, and the finest clay is mixed with quite large boulders in a completely disorderly fashion.

Sometimes the deposit is two-fold in nature, with a marked absence of boulders in the lower portion, which is altogether finer and more compacted. This is the debris that lay under the ice, the ground moraine. The debris from higher in the thickness of ice, includes boulders of all sizes, and, as melting occurred, this fell on top of the ground moraine as an unsorted mass.

This is the ground on which most of the farmers of Britain, excepting in the extreme south, have to work. The whole system of lowland agriculture is controlled by the small relief features and the soils that were produced by this glacial and meltwater deposition. When it is a true clay, the till is often a wet, cold soil, difficult to work. At other times it is much sandier and proves easy to plough. Near the mountains it is generally too stony to permit the use of any kind of tool more than a spade and crop-farming becomes almost impossible. Fig. 194 shows how attempts have been made in County Galway to clear the ground by piling the erratics up into numerous walls. The same has been done in many parts of New England.

Again, the places where deposits of sand and gravel with little clay occur (see page 110) are very favourable dry spots, either for buildings, as at Pickering (see Fig. 195), or for crops that require little moisture.

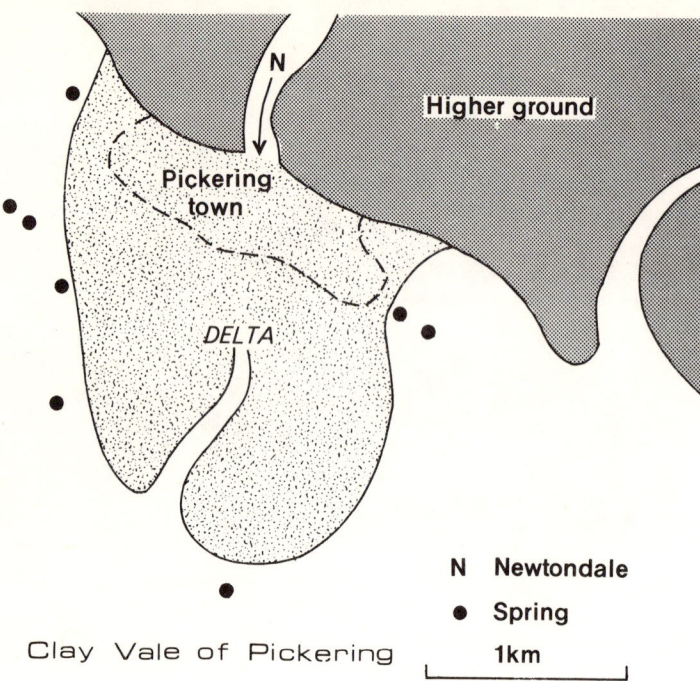

Higher ground

N Pickering town

DELTA

Clay Vale of Pickering

N Newtondale

• Spring

1km

It is very true to say that in one particular climate the farmer is very largely controlled by the physical geography of his land, and that he grows what he can, and not always what he wishes.

Fig. 195 Pickering is built on a gravel delta

Acknowledgements

The great majority of the photographs in this book have been taken from the collection of the late R. Kay Gresswell. Where this is not the case the source is indicated in the caption and acknowledgements are due to the various bodies quoted.

The diagrams have been drawn for this book by cartographers of the Geography Department, King's College London and I am grateful for their help.

G. R. P. L.